"I believe every single person in the audience of *The Writer* will have a story that puts them in the world of the play. Norm Foster puts us in that world with humour, seriousness, compassion, frustration and understanding. And just for fun, there is a bombshell of a revelation that will have your eyeballs popping . . . Foster gives Blake a speech to his father in Act II that is so true, so moving that it leaves one limp with emotion."

—Lynn Slotkin, *The Slotkin Letter*

"Foster is so talented and comic that he adroitly assigns lines to an unseen lady next door who has the house howling with laughter."

—Mike Keenan, *Niagara Now*

"*The Writer* provides a sometimes-gut-wrenching experience many of us have dealt with in our own lives and finds shafts of light and gentle humor throughout . . . *The Writer* is simply one of Norm Foster's best efforts."

—Mike Saunders, *Fine Music*

The Writer

Also by Norm Foster

Bedtime Stories
Dear Santa
Ethan Claymore
A Foster Christmas
The Foster Season
The Foursome
The Gentleman Clothier
Hilda's Yard
Jasper Station
Jenny's House of Joy
Jonas and Barry in the Home
Kiss the Moon, Kiss the Sun
The Ladies Foursome
The Long Weekend
The Melville Boys
Mending Fences
Ned Durango (with Leslie Arden)
Office Hours
Old Love
On a First Name Basis
One-Actmanship
Opening Night
Outlaw
Self-Help
Sinners
Skin Flick
Storm Warning
Triple Play
Wrong for Each Other

The Writer

NORM FOSTER

Playwrights Canada Press
TORONTO

Library and Archives Canada Cataloguing in Publication
Title: The writer / Norm Foster.
Names: Foster, Norm, 1949- author.
Description: A play.
Identifiers: Canadiana (print) 20200364286 | Canadiana (ebook) 20200364340 | ISBN 9780369101372 (softcover) | ISBN 9780369101389 (PDF) | ISBN 9780369101396 (EPUB) | ISBN 9780369101402 (Kindle)
Classification: LCC PS8561.O7745 W75 2020 | DDC C812/.54—dc23

Playwrights Canada Press operates on Mississaugas of the Credit, Wendat, Anishinaabe, Métis, and Haudenosaunee land. It always was and always will be Indigenous land.

We acknowledge the financial support of the Canada Council for the Arts—which last year invested $153 million to bring the arts to Canadians throughout the country—the Ontario Arts Council (OAC), Ontario Creates, and the Government of Canada for our publishing activities.

for Robert Brickell

The Writer was first produced at the Foster Festival in St. Catharines, Ontario, from June 19 to July 5, 2019, with the following cast and creative team:

Donald Wellner: Guy Bannerman
Blake Wellner: Jamie Williams

Director: Patricia Vanstone
Set and Costume Design: Peter Hartwell
Lighting Design: Chris Malkowski
Stage Manager: Carolyn MacKenzie
Apprentice Stage Manager: Melanie Coomber
Production Manager: David Costello

Characters

Donald Wellner
ages sixty-eight to seventy-five during the course of the play

Blake Wellner
ages forty-two to forty-nine during the course of the play

Place

The main living area of Donald Wellner's one-bedroom apartment. There is a small beer fridge in part of the room. There is also one couch and one chair. And there is a desk with an old typewriter on it. There is a door to the apartment and another door that leads to the bedroom and bathroom area and a third entrance that leads to the kitchen.

Act One

SCENE ONE

Seven years ago. October. Lights up. DONALD *Wellner enters from the kitchen. He is followed by* BLAKE *Wellner.*

DONALD: Oh, and I have a beer fridge too. See? I keep it out here because there's no room in the kitchen.

BLAKE: A beer fridge in the living room?

DONALD: I know. A dream come true. Would you like a beer?

BLAKE: Sure.

DONALD: Attaboy. The sun is over the yardarm, right?

DONALD *gets two cans of beer out of the beer fridge.*

BLAKE: So, you're okay with living here?

DONALD: Oh absolutely, yes.

BLAKE: Hmm.

DONALD: Why? What's wrong with it?

BLAKE: Well, it's a lot smaller than what you're used to. I mean, you're a rich man, Dad. I think you can afford to get a better place.

DONALD: Oh, this is just temporary.

BLAKE: It is?

DONALD: Oh, yes. Yes. Your mother and I will work things out. You'll see.

BLAKE: Dad, you don't rent an apartment if you think things are going to work out.

DONALD: It's a short-term rental.

BLAKE: Why didn't you go to a hotel?

DONALD: That would be even smaller. No, your mother and I will get past this in no time.

BLAKE: You think so?

DONALD: Oh, yes. We're already talking.

BLAKE: Are you?

DONALD: We spoke on the phone last night. Had a very positive conversation.

BLAKE: When she told you never to call her again? That conversation?

DONALD: That was only a small part of the conversation.

BLAKE: Dad, I was at Mom's last night. I heard the conversation. That was the conversation.

DONALD: No, look. Don't you worry. It'll work itself out.

BLAKE: I'm not worried. I'm forty-two years old. I'm beyond worrying what you and Mom do in your relationship. I just want you both to be happy. That's all I want.

DONALD: And we will be. We'll figure this out.

BLAKE: You're sixty-eight, Dad. Shouldn't you have life figured out by now?

DONALD: You never figure life out, Blake. That's what makes it so exciting. If I could figure life out, I wouldn't want to live it. You have to live each day as if you're riding a Brahma bull and you're about to get thrown off its back onto the humbling dirt below. That's how you live.

BLAKE: Do you think that's how Mom feels?

DONALD: Your mother is different. She likes being settled. She doesn't like surprises.

BLAKE: And you do?

DONALD: I like not knowing what's around the next corner.

BLAKE: Uh-huh. Well, you're probably better off that way because I have a feeling that around the next corner is an eighteen-wheeler coming at you head-on. I see you're still writing on this old Underwood.

DONALD: I wrote *A Kind Heart* on that typewriter. That's my lucky typewriter.

BLAKE: You wrote one hit play on this typewriter thirty-five years ago. And that makes it your lucky typewriter?

DONALD: Hey, *A Kind Heart* put you and your sister through university. It put a roof over your head. A damn nice roof. So don't knock my typewriter.

BLAKE: All right. Don't get excited. So, what are you working on these days?

BLAKE reads the sheet of paper that's in the typewriter.

Cast in Stone.

DONALD: A very provocative piece. Filled with angst, intrigue, and unrequited love. It will shine a light on social injustice across the land.

BLAKE: Page one.

DONALD: Just getting started. But, I think it's an important play. It'll make people think.

BLAKE: An important play. Just what the world needs.

DONALD: You know, I wish you wouldn't mock me like that, Blake.

BLAKE: I'm not mocking you.

DONALD: You are mocking me.

BLAKE: All right, maybe a little bit.

DONALD: And you have no right to mock. You have no idea what goes on in a writer's mind.

BLAKE: Dad, I'm a writer.

DONALD: A travel writer.

BLAKE: And that's not writing?

DONALD: That's reporting. That's not creating.

BLAKE: Thanks, Dad.

DONALD: Well, isn't it? You get on a plane, you fly someplace, and you say, "Oh look. The pyramids." And then you write about the pyramids. The pyramids have been there for thousands of years, Blake. You didn't create the pyramids. You're reporting on the pyramids. Then you get on another plane and you say, "Oh, look. Stonehenge." And you write about Stonehenge. It is nothing like what I do.

BLAKE: What you did, Dad. What you did.

DONALD: What do you mean?

BLAKE: You wrote one play.

DONALD: I've written many plays.

BLAKE: Okay. I'm sorry. One play that's been produced.

DONALD: All over the world, I might add. Nine hundred and forty-eight performances on Broadway. Two years on the West End. Touring productions as far away as Australia. Revival upon revival. Production after production.

BLAKE: Dad, I'm your son. Please don't recite your resumé to me.

DONALD: I just want to make sure you don't forget it.

BLAKE: I won't forget it. Believe me. It's like a shadow on my chest X-ray.

DONALD: And well it should be. That was a joke.

BLAKE: I know. I love you, Dad.

DONALD: I love you too, son.

BLAKE: God.

DONALD: So, do you want to stay and watch the football game with me? There's a football game on today.

BLAKE: You don't have a TV.

DONALD: There's a TV in the bedroom. We can watch it in there. And I've got potato chips. Barbecue. Your favourite.

BLAKE: Tempting, but no, I can't.

DONALD: Come on. It'll be like old times. We used to watch football together every Sunday. Remember that? The National Football League. The league of my people.

BLAKE: Your people?

DONALD: The Americans.

BLAKE: I would hardly call them your people, Dad. You were born there, yes, but your parents moved you here when you were two.

DONALD: They ripped me from my homeland. I was devastated.

BLAKE: You were two.

DONALD: I was very advanced for my age. Now, stay. Watch the game with me.

BLAKE: Dad, I can't. Mom's cooking dinner for us today.

DONALD: Oh. I see.

BLAKE: I'm sorry.

DONALD: No, that's fine. It's good that you're there for you mother. That's good. She needs you right now. What about Mandy? Is she going to be there too?

BLAKE: Yeah.

DONALD: Good. She'll be surrounded by love, your mother. That's good.

BLAKE: Have you spoken to Mandy since . . .

DONALD: No.

BLAKE: Well, she's pretty upset.

DONALD: I know. But she'll come around. This whole thing is going to blow over. You'll see.

BLAKE: You think so?

DONALD: Oh yes. It's minor. It'll blow right over. Mandy can't stay mad at her old man. A father-daughter relationship is very special. We'll patch it up.

BLAKE: Well, she is your favourite.

DONALD: Oh, don't start that again. I have no favourite.

BLAKE: No?

DONALD: No. I've always treated you and your sister exactly the same. There's been no favouritism on either side.

BLAKE: Well, I don't know about that.

DONALD: There hasn't. You can ask your mother.

BLAKE: No, Mom saw it too, Dad. So did Mandy.

DONALD: Oh, that's nonsense.

BLAKE: All right. Whatever.

DONALD: So, how long are you in town for this time?

BLAKE: Just until tomorrow night.

DONALD: And then where are you off to?

BLAKE: Chile. I'm doing a piece on the marble caves.

DONALD: You travel too much.

BLAKE: Well, that's my job.

DONALD: But I don't get to see you. I see you whenever you have a layover. You're never around more than two days at a time.

BLAKE: I know. I'm sorry.

DONALD: I barely know what's going on in your life.

BLAKE: Travel is what's going on in my life. So far this year I've visited ninety-five different locations.

DONALD: Ninety-five?

BLAKE: Yes. That's all I do. I get on a plane and I get off a plane. That's my life.

DONALD: It doesn't sound like much of a life.

BLAKE: I have to earn money, Dad. In fact, most travel writers have second jobs to keep us afloat.

DONALD: And what's your second job?

BLAKE: I write a restaurant column for the *Herald*.

DONALD: A food critic?

BLAKE: Yeah.

DONALD: I thought you were a travel writer. Why didn't you tell me you wrote a food column?

BLAKE: I only tell you things that I think will impress you.

DONALD: And you thought "travel writer" would do that?

BLAKE: Anyway, the restaurant column is in the paper every Saturday.

DONALD: Well, I'll have to buy a *Herald* and have a look. First thing tomorrow.

BLAKE: I'm sorry I'm not around very much. I'll call more often. How's that?

DONALD: That would be the very least you could do. And how's that woman you've been seeing?

BLAKE: What woman?

DONALD: The lawyer.

BLAKE: What lawyer?

DONALD: Weren't you seeing a lawyer?

BLAKE: I was seeing a lawyer, yes. I wasn't dating a lawyer. And it was a man. It wasn't a woman.

DONALD: So, you're gay? Your mother and I always wondered about that.

BLAKE: No, Dad. I'm not gay.

DONALD: Is that why you don't watch football anymore?

BLAKE: I do watch football.

DONALD: Just because you're gay doesn't mean you can't watch football.

BLAKE: I'm not gay! And I do watch football!

DONALD: Hey, don't get defensive. I don't care if you're gay.

BLAKE: I'm not getting defensive. If I was gay I would tell you. It wouldn't bother me.

DONALD: Good. Because it doesn't bother me either. I work in the theatre.

BLAKE: Oh my God. Dad, I was seeing a lawyer because I'm having a will drawn up.

DONALD: Oh.

BLAKE: Do you understand now?

DONALD: Completely. Yes.

BLAKE: Good.

DONALD: Is he a nice man?

BLAKE: Who?

DONALD: This lawyer you're seeing.

BLAKE: Yes. He's a wonderful man.

DONALD: Then that's all that matters.

BLAKE: But I'm not seeing him in that way.

DONALD: In what way? Seeing who?

BLAKE: The lawyer. Dad, are you okay?

DONALD: Okay how?

BLAKE: You know? Just . . . okay. Are you feeling all right?

DONALD: I'm feeling fine.

BLAKE: Are you sure?

DONALD: Of course I'm sure. I'm fine.

BLAKE: All right.

DONALD: I've never felt better.

BLAKE: Really?

DONALD: No. God. I'm sixty-eight. Of course I've felt better. In fact, I've never felt worse. I ache everywhere. I groan when I stand up. I groan when I sit down. Sometimes I groan when I'm not moving at all. I'll hear a groan and I'll think, "What the hell was that?" And it was me. Groaning. I groan for no reason.

BLAKE: You need to exercise. Start moving around. Get your joints loosened up.

DONALD: Do you exercise?

BLAKE: Oh God no. But I hear it's good for you.

DONALD: It is good for you. I used to exercise quite a bit when I was younger.

BLAKE: Then start exercising again. I'm worried about you, Dad. You know? Because of this whole thing with Mom. I'm worried that you're giving up on yourself.

DONALD: Oh, no. Not at all. And this thing with your mother, it's fine. It's just a little speed bump.

BLAKE: So, do you want to tell me what happened?

DONALD: Why are you having a will drawn up?

BLAKE: Because everyone should have a will. Don't you have a will?

DONALD: Of course I have a will. But I have things to leave and people to leave them to. You have no children, no mate. You have no possessions. You're practically a hobo. You're Mister Bojangles.

BLAKE: I am not a hobo. I have possessions.

DONALD: You live in an apartment.

BLAKE: You live in an apartment.

DONALD: It's temporary!

BLAKE: Well, I'm having a will drawn up so that my stuff, what there is of it, doesn't wind up in strangers' hands.

DONALD: What are you leaving me?

BLAKE: Leaving you? What? You think I'm going to die before you?

DONALD: Well, you travel a lot.

BLAKE: So?

DONALD: So, what if a plane goes down? What if you get stepped on by an elephant? Or gored by a wildebeest. I mean, what's the worst that can happen to me? My chair tips over.

BLAKE: What would you like me to leave you?

DONALD: Your Pulitzer Prize. Oh, wait. You don't have one. I have one. Sorry.

BLAKE: Asshole.

They laugh about this.

Did I ever tell you how proud I am of you for winning that?

DONALD: Oh, I'm sure you did.

BLAKE: Well, I am. Very proud.

DONALD: Thank you.

BLAKE: So, are you going to tell me what happened or not?

DONALD: Happened where? You mean with your mother and me?

BLAKE: Yes.

DONALD: Your mother didn't tell you?

BLAKE: There are two sides to every story, Dad. I want to hear yours.

DONALD: Well, quite honestly there isn't much to tell.

BLAKE: No?

DONALD: Hardly anything at all. You see, there was this actress . . .

BLAKE: Oh, God.

DONALD: What's wrong?

BLAKE: No story that begins with "there was this actress" ever ends well.

DONALD: Would you just listen please? Her name was Virginia Honeywell. She was starring in the West End production of *A Kind Heart* thirty-three years ago in London. I went over there for the rehearsals.

BLAKE: Yes, I remember you going to London.

DONALD: During rehearsals, her husband died unexpectedly. She was crushed, of course, but she stayed with the show nonetheless.

BLAKE: The show must go on, right?

DONALD: Right. She also discovered that before he died her husband had gambled away their life savings and she had nothing to live on. She was destitute. So, I helped her out.

BLAKE: Helped her out how?

DONALD: I paid her rent for her. Nothing more. That was it. Just the rent. I did it to ease her burden.

BLAKE: Were you in love with this actress?

DONALD: . . . Maybe just a little.

BLAKE: Oh, Dad.

DONALD: But I never acted on it. I was married. And she was newly widowed. The timing made it impossible.

BLAKE: The timing?

DONALD: Yes.

BLAKE: So, if things were different, if the timing was right—meaning if you weren't married to Mom—you would have pursued a relationship with this actress?

DONALD: I think I would have, yes.

BLAKE: Boy. That brings up a lot of questions.

DONALD: Like what?

BLAKE: Well, did you resent Mom for that? Did you love this woman more than Mom?

DONALD: No, no, no. It wasn't like that at all. I loved your mother very much. I loved Virginia a little bit. There are different degrees of love.

BLAKE: Kind of like the way you love me as opposed to the way you love Mandy?

DONALD: You sound like a hurt little child, Blake. I told you. I have no favourite. I love you both equally. Although if you keep whining about it, Mandy could pull ahead.

BLAKE: So, how long did you pay the rent for this actress?

DONALD: Until she died.

BLAKE: And when was that?

DONALD: Two weeks ago.

BLAKE: What?!

DONALD: And through different channels, bank records, et cetera, it got back to your mother that I was paying her rent. She didn't tell you this?

BLAKE: She told me you had an affair with a British woman.

DONALD: And that's not true. That is not true at all. But I can certainly see how your mother might jump to that conclusion.

BLAKE: Because you've been paying her rent for thirty-three years? Yes, I can see that too. Why did you pay her rent for thirty-three years?

DONALD: It's complicated. But like I say, it eased her burden considerably, and I was happy to do that.

BLAKE: You didn't have a child with this woman, did you? Is that why you paid her rent?

DONALD: No. Absolutely not. The relationship was strictly above board. Strictly platonic.

BLAKE: Well, good luck convincing Mom of that.

DONALD: No, it'll be fine.

BLAKE: You paid her rent for thirty-three years? How much money would that be?

DONALD: I have no idea.

BLAKE: If her rent was even two thousand pounds a month that would be twenty-four thousand pounds a year. Times thirty-three years, that's . . . that's almost eight hundred thousand pounds.

DONALD: I've never sat down and added it up, so I don't know.

BLAKE: Dad?

DONALD: It eased her burden. That's all I cared about. So, please, let's hear no more about it.

BLAKE: Wow.

DONALD: No more.

BLAKE: All right. I won't mention it again.

DONALD: Thank you. So, I guess this means I won't be getting any grandchildren from you.

BLAKE: What? Why?

DONALD: Because you're gay.

BLAKE: I'm not gay.

DONALD: Your mother thinks you're gay.

BLAKE: She does not. Does she?

DONALD: She's mentioned it several times. I mean, you're forty-two. You have no girlfriend. Even if you weren't gay, it's a little late to meet someone and start a family now. So, you might as well just go ahead and be gay.

BLAKE: Maybe I don't want a family.

DONALD: What? You don't want a family?

BLAKE: Maybe I don't.

DONALD: Then you shouldn't have one. If you're not sure about it then you shouldn't take that leap. A family is a very big step in a man's life. You can't go into it half-heartedly.

BLAKE: Finally, some fatherly advice.

DONALD: That's what I'm here for. And don't worry about giving us grandchildren. We'll let that burden fall on Mandy's shoulders.

BLAKE: Mandy's thirty-nine and has no man in her life.

DONALD: Is Mandy gay too? How blind can I be?

BLAKE: Mandy's not gay. Mandy and I . . . I don't know. Relationships aren't essential to us. We have other interests.

DONALD: It doesn't matter what other interests you have, Blake. It's not natural to go through life alone. You need a partner to share in the highs and the lows.

BLAKE: If it happens, it happens. If it doesn't, I'm okay with it.

DONALD: All right. To each his own, I guess.

BLAKE: Thank you.

DONALD: But it's not natural. Can you stay for lunch at least?

BLAKE looks at his watch.

BLAKE: Uh . . . yeah, I can stay for lunch.

DONALD: Good.

BLAKE: In fact, let me make you some lunch.

DONALD: No, you don't have to do that. I've got sandwich meat in there.

BLAKE: No, I want to do it, Dad. Come on. I found a great recipe in Turkey last month. It's called karniyarik. Eggplant stuffed with sautéed onions, garlic, black pepper, tomatoes, green pepper, parsley, and ground beef.

DONALD: That sounds good.

BLAKE: You'll love it. I'll go to the grocery store down the street and buy what I need.

DONALD: Let me give you some money.

BLAKE: No. This is on me.

DONALD: Are you sure?

BLAKE: I'm positive. Why don't you have a nap? When you wake up, I'll have your lunch ready for you.

DONALD: No. I'll only nap until you get back from the grocery store. But then I'm getting up. I want to spend time with you. I hardly see you anymore.

BLAKE: Okay. You go and lie down. I'll wake you when I get back. Okay?

DONALD: Okay.

BLAKE: Good.

DONALD: I hardly see you, Blake. I miss you.

BLAKE: I know Dad. I miss you too. Hey, maybe I can watch the first half of the football game with you.

DONALD: That would be wonderful.

BLAKE: Now go and lie down. I'll be back in fifteen minutes.

DONALD: All right, son. Blake?

BLAKE stops.

You're a good boy. A good son.

BLAKE: Go lie down.

BLAKE exits.

DONALD: *(to himself)* Go lie down. Like I'm a dog he orders me.

DONALD heads to the bedroom but then stops and looks at his typewriter.

(to himself) Very important play.

DONALD exits to the bedroom. Lights down.

SCENE TWO

Six years ago. August.

Lights come up and we hear BLAKE and DONALD off stage. They are bringing a piece of furniture into the apartment.

DONALD: *(off)* Wait. Wait. We should flip it on its side.

BLAKE: *(off)* Why should we flip it on its side?

DONALD: *(off)* Because that's what you do with furniture. When you're moving furniture you always flip it on its side.

BLAKE: *(off)* It's fine like this. Are you ready?

DONALD: *(off)* Ready.

BLAKE: *(off)* Okay. Lift.

BLAKE and DONALD enter. They are carrying a bookcase.

Where do you want it?

DONALD: Uh . . . over there.

BLAKE and DONALD move the bookcase to where DONALD indicated, and they set it down.

There. Perfect.

BLAKE: It looks good.

DONALD: It does, doesn't it?

BLAKE: It fills up that space nicely.

DONALD: Very nice.

BLAKE looks around.

BLAKE: Dad? Is that the first piece of furniture you've bought since you moved in last year?

DONALD: Yes, it is.

BLAKE: Why wouldn't you buy more? The place is practically empty.

DONALD: Well, you know.

BLAKE: You thought this was just going to be temporary. You thought Mom would take you back.

DONALD: I thought she would, yes.

BLAKE: I told you last year that wasn't going to happen.

DONALD: I'm an optimist. In fact, I still hold out hope.

BLAKE: Really?

DONALD: Yes. We spoke on the phone last week, your mother and me. Had a very positive conversation.

BLAKE: Uh-huh. What about Mandy?

DONALD: Well, Mandy's a tough nut. She's like her old man. But she'll come around.

BLAKE: Dad, it's been almost a year. I talk to Mandy all the time. I know how she feels. And she has no intention of reconciling with you.

DONALD: Oh, don't count me out yet, Blake. I've got the Wellner charm working in my favour. That bookcase needs a book.

DONALD moves to the desk where his typewriter sits. He opens a drawer and pulls out a book.

BLAKE: Good idea. Nothing like a bookcase full of books to make a person appear intellectual.

DONALD: What do you mean "appear" intellectual. I am intellectual. I won the Pulitzer Prize for God's sake.

DONALD puts the book on the bookcase then stands back and admires it.

There we go. Now it's a bookcase.

BLAKE: One book?

DONALD: What's wrong?

BLAKE: Aren't you going to put more books on there?

DONALD: I don't have more books. I have one book.

BLAKE: Then why did you buy a bookcase?

DONALD: What writer doesn't have a bookcase?

BLAKE: What writer doesn't have books?

DONALD: I don't read books. You know that.

BLAKE: Again then, why the bookcase?

DONALD: Every home needs a bookcase, Blake. Don't worry. I'll fill it with family photos.

BLAKE: You have family photos?

DONALD: I've got a box of them in the bedroom.

BLAKE: Where did you get those?

DONALD: From your mother. That's what we were discussing on the phone last week. I called her and asked if I could have some of the family photos and she said yes.

BLAKE: So, you went to the house? You saw Mom?

DONALD: No. No. She had a friend drop them off to me.

BLAKE: Which friend?

DONALD: Polly Amherst.

BLAKE: Polly Amherst. I don't know a Polly Amherst.

DONALD: Well, Polly is actually a friend of a friend of your mother's.

BLAKE: I don't understand.

DONALD: Your mother didn't want to see me, so she asked a friend of hers, Jane Kinsey, to drop the photos off to me.

BLAKE: I know Jane.

DONALD: Lovely woman.

BLAKE: Very sweet.

DONALD: She's got a big heart.

BLAKE: She's adorable.

DONALD: But Jane can't stand the sight of me either, so she asked a friend of hers to drop the photos off.

BLAKE: Polly Amherst.

DONALD: Right.

BLAKE: Good God, Dad. And you're optimistic about patching things up with Mom? She's passing possessions to you through channels like it's the Underground Railroad.

DONALD: Even the darkest night will end, and the sun will rise.

BLAKE: Victor Hugo.

DONALD: *Les Misérables.* Very good. I've taught you well.

BLAKE: I learned that in school.

DONALD: No, I'm pretty sure you learned that from the old man.

BLAKE: You don't read books. How would you know a line from *Les Misérables*?

DONALD: I sat through the musical once. Longest hour of my life.

BLAKE: That show is three hours long.

DONALD: I didn't say I sat through it all.

BLAKE takes the book off of the bookcase, looks at it, and reads the cover.

BLAKE: *A Kind Heart.* This is the book you put on the bookshelf? Your own play?

DONALD: It'll be a reminder to me.

BLAKE: A reminder of what?

DONALD: Of the heights I once climbed. I'll leave it there and as I work at my desk on my latest project, it will be an inspiration to me. I think I'll get those photos out.

DONALD exits to the bedroom. BLAKE goes to the desk and looks at the piece of paper in the typewriter. DONALD enters carrying a box.

Here we go.

BLAKE: Dad?

DONALD: Yes?

BLAKE: Your latest project. You're still on page one.

DONALD: Because this project cannot be rushed. This is the one that will put me back on top. I've got to take my time with it.

BLAKE: But you haven't written anything in a year.

DONALD: I'm thinking about it. Running the story through my head over and over. And when I'm ready, I will sit down at the typewriter and it will flow out of me. This is how a writer works, Blake. You wouldn't know about that.

BLAKE: God. Dad, I'm a writer too!

DONALD: Yes. And how is that food column coming along? I meant to buy a newspaper when you mentioned it to me.

BLAKE: I mentioned it to you last year.

DONALD: No, it was just the other day.

BLAKE: Dad, it was last year.

DONALD: No, I don't think so.

BLAKE: Dad?

DONALD: Fine! Last year! Yesterday. What does it matter? I forgot because I've been busy with the new play.

BLAKE: You're still on page one.

DONALD holds up a framed photograph.

DONALD: Oh, look. Remember this? This is the four of us at Lake Murdoch. Remember that? That was a wonderful weekend. You were probably seven years old and Mandy must've been four. Look at her there. She was so cute. We rented a cabin and you and Mandy slept on the pullout in the living room and your mother and I took the bedroom. We made love all night long.

BLAKE: Oh, jeez, Dad!

DONALD: What's wrong? We did.

BLAKE: My God.

DONALD: This was just before *A Kind Heart* opened. We had no idea how our lives were about to change. Well, this deserves a place on the bookshelf for sure. Yes. There we go.

DONALD puts the photo on the bookshelf. He takes another photograph out of the box.

Let's see what else we have here.

BLAKE: And please spare me the lurid backstory on any other photos, okay?

DONALD: Oh, look at this. You know what that is?

DONALD shows BLAKE the photo.

BLAKE: It's all the Pulitzer Prize winners at the awards luncheon.

DONALD: There I am there. That was a magnificent day. They put your mother and I up in the finest hotel in New York. That was another wonderful night of lovemaking.

BLAKE: Dad, please, you're killing my childhood.

DONALD: I'll put this right up here beside the Lake Murdoch photo. Such great memories. And I'm only two photos in. Now, what else?

DONALD reaches into the box. He pulls out a photo.

Oh, look at this. Mandy's graduation from medical school. I flew in from Warsaw to be there for the ceremony. Oh, I wasn't going to miss that, her being the valedictorian and all. I still remember her smiling at me from the podium. That's a smile I will never forget.

DONALD puts the photo on the bookshelf. While he is doing that, BLAKE takes a photo out of the box.

BLAKE: Here's my little league baseball photo.

DONALD: Oh yes. Look at you. The bat on your shoulder, poised to take a mighty swing.

BLAKE: I remember you said they should have taken a photo of me sitting on the bench because that's where I spent most of my time.

DONALD: Oh, I was just kidding.

BLAKE: Were you?

DONALD: Well, not entirely.

DONALD puts the photo on the bookcase. BLAKE takes another photo out of the box.

BLAKE: Dad?

DONALD: What?

BLAKE shows DONALD the photo. DONALD is stopped by it.

Oh.

BLAKE: Your wedding photo.

DONALD: That was taken on the steps of the church. Three o'clock in the afternoon. You can see the shadows that are being cast behind us. Your mother's head is lowered slightly because she didn't like the idea of being photographed up like that. She always knows what her best look is.

BLAKE: Mom gave you your wedding photo?

DONALD: Well, I'm sure she has a copy.

BLAKE: You think so?

DONALD: Oh, she must, yes. Or maybe she put this in here by mistake. That's probably what happened. I'll call her this evening and let her know that I have it.

DONALD sets the photo on the bookcase.

BLAKE: Dad . . .

DONALD: You know what? I can put these photos up later. Right now, I want to spend time with my son, who I never see.

DONALD picks up the box of photos and exits to the bedroom with it. There is a pause.

BLAKE: Dad?

There is no answer.

Dad, are you okay?

DONALD enters. He is obviously a little upset. Maybe wiping away a tear but putting up a brave front.

DONALD: I'm fine. Yes. I think seeing those photographs was a little emotional for me, that's all. You and Mandy . . . Our family. I didn't see that coming. You know what? Let me buy you lunch.

BLAKE: No, you don't have to do that.

DONALD: No, I want to. How often do I get to buy my son the food critic some lunch? Hey, you can suggest the best place to eat, right? Mister food critic.

DONALD grabs a jacket from somewhere in the room.

BLAKE: The food critic thing is just my second job, Dad. Travel writing is where I excel.

DONALD: Well, as long as you excel at something. Now, where do you suggest we go?

BLAKE: Uh . . . The Marigold is good. And it's within walking distance.

DONALD: Then the Marigold it is. Oh, this is very exciting, yes. Will they know who you are at the Marigold? Will you get special treatment?

BLAKE: Probably not.

DONALD: Well, give it time, Blake. Don't get discouraged because you haven't made a name for yourself yet. It'll happen.

BLAKE: I'm not discouraged.

DONALD: That's the spirit, son.

BLAKE: I'm feeling very good about myself.

DONALD: And why shouldn't you?

BLAKE: No, really, Dad. I am.

DONALD: And I believe you.

BLAKE: Do you?

DONALD: Yes. You're telling me you feel good about yourself. Why wouldn't I believe you? Now, let's go. Should we make a reservation, or do you have some influence there?

BLAKE: Well . . .

DONALD: No, we should make a reservation. You can call on the way down. My son the food critic. I'm so proud.

DONALD and BLAKE exit. Lights down.

SCENE THREE

Five years ago. August.

Lights come up and we hear BLAKE *and* DONALD *off stage. They are bringing a piece of furniture into the apartment.*

DONALD: *(off)* Flip it on its side.

BLAKE: *(off)* Dad, we don't need to flip it on its side. It's fine.

DONALD: *(off)* I think it'll be easier if it's flipped on its side.

BLAKE: *(off)* No, look. It's in already. It's already in. It's good.

DONALD and BLAKE enter. They are carrying an easy chair.

DONALD: We should have flipped it on its side.

BLAKE: Do you want to take it back out and bring it in again by flipping it on its side?

DONALD: Well, that would be silly, wouldn't it? It's already in.

BLAKE: Then stop saying we should flip it on its side. Where do you want it?

DONALD: Right here.

They set the chair down.

There. Good. And one final adjustment.

DONALD turns the chair slightly so that it is facing his desk and typewriter.

And perfect.

BLAKE: What was that for?

DONALD: I want it facing my work.

BLAKE: Why? You should have it facing the window.

DONALD: No. This way when I'm lounging in the chair of an afternoon, maybe having a beverage or two, I will be looking at my workstation and thinking about what's to come. I will be willing the story to take shape. Now, that might not work for some writers, but for me it does. You see, Blake, writers work in different ways. There is no right or wrong way. Whatever works for the individual writer.

BLAKE: I know.

DONALD: How would you know?

BLAKE: I'm a writer!

DONALD: Of course you are. Can I get you a beer, son? You've earned it.

BLAKE: Sure. Thanks.

DONALD goes to the beer fridge and takes out two beers. BLAKE moves to the typewriter and looks at the paper in the carriage.

Page eight?

DONALD: What's that?

BLAKE: *Cast in Stone.* You're on page eight.

DONALD: Yes.

BLAKE: Where are the other seven pages?

DONALD: In the desk drawer. I never leave completed pages lying around. It gives one a sense of accomplishment and I don't want to feel that until the entire script is completed.

BLAKE: Can I read what you've got so far?

DONALD hands BLAKE a can of beer.

DONALD: No. Good heavens no. I never show a script to anyone until the first draft is finished. I don't want to be influenced by outside opinions.

DONALD sits in the new easy chair.

Ahhh. This is lovely. Sit, son. Sit.

BLAKE sits on the couch. DONALD's chair is facing away from BLAKE.

So, tell me what's new in your life.

BLAKE: Well, it's funny you should ask, Dad, because I've got some news.

DONALD: Really? And what news would that be?

BLAKE: Well . . . Dad, this isn't working.

DONALD: What's not working?

BLAKE: I can't . . . Turn your chair around.

DONALD: Oh. All right.

DONALD turns the chair around and sits again.

Oh, that's much better.

BLAKE: Do you think so?

DONALD: Oh, a big improvement, yes.

BLAKE: I thought it might be.

DONALD: This has been nice having you in town for an entire week, Blake. I don't realize how much I miss you until you're actually here. Then it dawns on me how much time you spend on the road.

BLAKE: Well, that's what my news is about.

DONALD: How's your mother?

BLAKE: Uh . . . Mom's fine. She's started giving singing lessons. At home. She has about five students already.

DONALD: Singing lessons? Why would she do that? She doesn't need to work. I send her money every month.

BLAKE: She's doing it because she wants to. It's a skill she has that she wants to pass on. That's all.

DONALD: But she's not hurting for money, is she?

BLAKE: No, not at all. You've been more than generous considering there is no formal separation agreement in place.

DONALD: Good. But you'll tell me if she's hurting financially.

BLAKE: I'll tell you.

DONALD: That woman is a beautiful singer. She had a very nice career going once. But she gave it up to raise you and your sister.

BLAKE: I know.

DONALD: Not that I want to make you feel guilty about that.

BLAKE: Of course not.

DONALD: I just want to make sure you're aware of the sacrifices we made for you.

BLAKE: I'm aware.

DONALD: If you want to feel guilty, that's your choice. A compassionate person would feel guilty, that's all I'm saying.

BLAKE: Can I tell you my news now?

DONALD: You know what? Have a look at the first seven pages.

DONALD goes to the desk and takes out the seven pages of his script.

BLAKE: Really?

DONALD: Yes. Why not? What's the harm? It might be good to get a second opinion from a layman.

BLAKE: Well, I'm not really a layman.

DONALD: What's that?

BLAKE: I'm not really a layman because I'm a . . . never mind.

DONALD: You know, sometimes I get so wrapped up in my writing I can't see the forest for the trees. Maybe you can point out something that I'm missing. There. Give it a quick read.

DONALD hands the script to BLAKE.

BLAKE: Now?

DONALD: Yes, now. It's only seven pages.

BLAKE: All right.

DONALD: I'll just . . . I'll stand back here. I won't hover. You go ahead and read.

BLAKE: Okay.

DONALD: Take your time. That's page one right there.

BLAKE: I know it's page one. It says page one at the top.

DONALD: Good. I just want to be certain you're reading it in the correct order.

BLAKE: I am. Don't worry.

DONALD: And be harsh. Don't pull any punches. I can take it.

DONALD moves upstage. BLAKE starts to read. After a moment, he speaks.

BLAKE: There's a typo on page one.

DONALD: What?

BLAKE: A typo. I think it should say "he cares for me" and it says "he cars for me." You left out the "e."

DONALD: A typo?

BLAKE: Yeah. Look.

BLAKE holds up the page.

See?

DONALD: You're critiquing my work?

BLAKE: No, I'm just pointing out a typo.

DONALD: What gives you the right to critique my work? You're not a writer.

BLAKE: I AM a writer.

DONALD: Yes, you keep saying that. Give me that.

DONALD grabs the script.

I should have known better than to let you read it.

DONALD puts the script back in the desk drawer.

But you insisted. I won't make that mistake again.

BLAKE: I didn't insist. And you said you wanted me to point out things that you might've missed.

DONALD: And you went right for the jugular.

BLAKE: I pointed out a typo.

DONALD: And you took great pleasure in that, didn't you?

BLAKE: Oh my God. Dad, can I tell you my news now?

DONALD: Certainly. Go right ahead. Or is it more criticism of my work? In which case I don't want to hear it.

BLAKE: It's got nothing to do with your work.

DONALD: Well, that'll be a breath of fresh air. A break from your constant condemnation of my craft.

BLAKE: Would you sit down, please?

DONALD: Why?

BLAKE: So I can tell you my news.

DONALD: It's sit-down news?

BLAKE: I think it is, yes.

DONALD: I don't like sit-down news. It's never good. No one ever says "sit down" when you've won the lottery. They say sit down when you've got a tumour.

BLAKE: Dad, please. Just sit.

DONALD: Fine. But I won't like it.

DONALD sits in his chair, facing away from BLAKE.

All right. What's the news?

BLAKE: Would you turn around and face me, please?

DONALD: What?

BLAKE: Your chair. Turn it around.

DONALD turns the chair around.

DONALD: Oh, that's better.

BLAKE: Dad, I'm moving away.

DONALD: What do you mean moving away? Moving away to where?

BLAKE: London.

DONALD: London? You're moving to London?

BLAKE: Yeah. I'm in town for this long right now because I'm packing up my stuff.

DONALD: When do you leave?

BLAKE: Day after tomorrow.

DONALD: Day after . . . why are you just telling me this now? You've been here for a week. Why couldn't you tell me before this?

BLAKE: I didn't know how. I mean, God, you're all alone here in this stupid apartment. You don't have any friends. You don't do anything. I'm basically your only contact with the outside world. And to tell you I'm moving away? I didn't want to do that to you.

DONALD: Oh, that's nonsense.

BLAKE: It's not nonsense, Dad.

DONALD: It is complete nonsense. I'm not all alone. I am in constant touch with my agent. And I have a friend across the hall. Roman . . . something.

BLAKE: You see? This is why I didn't know how to tell you. Dad, I think you're lost here.

DONALD: Lost?

BLAKE: Yes. You're fading into nothing in this apartment.

DONALD: Nothing? Well, I've got seven pages of script over there that says different.

BLAKE: You haven't put any more photos out. It's been a year. Why haven't you put more photos onto the bookcase?

DONALD: I haven't gotten around to it.

BLAKE: Because it hurts.

DONALD: No, that's not it.

BLAKE: It is too. All those memories? It hurts for you to look at those photographs.

DONALD: Well, of course it hurts!! Do you think I'm so insensitive that it doesn't hurt me to look at photos of the life I used to have? It hurts like hell. But I get through it. We always get through it. We have to. We have to keep moving forward. It's like a running back in football. Even when he's tied up, he keeps those legs pumping. Trying to move forward. If we don't move forward we stagnate. We die. I refuse to do that. So, please don't worry about me. All right?

BLAKE: I am worried about you.

DONALD: Well, don't. I'm working. I'm busy. I feel very much alive.

BLAKE: All right. I'm sorry. I didn't mean to excite you. You're working. You're on page eight. Good.

DONALD: Of a very important piece.

BLAKE: Very important. I know.

DONALD: And please don't use that mocking tone.

BLAKE: There's no tone. I'm not mocking.

DONALD: And see that you don't.

BLAKE: Fine.

DONALD: . . . We shouldn't fight, Blake. You're here so seldom, we shouldn't waste our time fighting when you're here. It's bad enough I've lost Mandy. I don't want the same to happen with you.

BLAKE: It won't. Don't worry.

DONALD: So, no more fighting. And no more mocking. All right?

BLAKE: All right.

DONALD: Good. So, why are you moving to London? Do you want to be closer to Stonehenge?

BLAKE: Now who's mocking?

DONALD: It's the Wellner wit. It can't be controlled. So why are you moving?

BLAKE: I got a job writing a travel column for the *Daily Telegraph*. They like my writing style because of the humour I employ.

DONALD: Ah, you see? The Wellner wit strikes again.

BLAKE: And there's talk that they might even syndicate the column somewhere down the road. I would be in newspapers all over the world.

DONALD: Well, look at you. Why, you'll be as famous as your old man.

BLAKE: No. That's never going to happen, Dad.

DONALD: Oh, I don't know about that.

BLAKE: I'll always be known as the son of the man who wrote *A Kind Heart*.

DONALD: Well, there are worse things.

BLAKE: You know what? There certainly are.

DONALD: So. London, huh?

BLAKE: Yeah. It's centrally located. I can hop over to all of the other European countries and Asia a lot easier from there.

DONALD: I spent some time in London myself.

BLAKE: I know you did.

DONALD: It was during the West End run of *A Kind Heart*.

BLAKE: I know that, Dad.

DONALD: Yes, that was quite the time. I enjoyed London very much.

BLAKE: Dad, can we talk about moving you out of here sometime soon?

DONALD: Moving me out? Why? I'm happy here.

BLAKE: Dad. Come on. You're better than this. You could be living in a penthouse somewhere. Or in a hotel. You could have housekeeping services. Fine restaurants right downstairs. You're not eating well here.

DONALD: I'm eating just fine.

BLAKE: You're not. I've seen your kitchen. You've got junk in there. Peanut butter. White bread. Store-bought butter tarts. That's not good for a man your age.

DONALD: I'm only seventy.

BLAKE: You're not "only" seventy, Dad. You're seventy. When you reach the age of seventy you stop putting "only" in front of it. You need some fruit. Some vegetables.

DONALD: You know I stayed at the Embassy West Hotel for five weeks when they were rehearsing *A Kind Heart* in New York. A wonderful hotel. Marvellous staff.

BLAKE: They tore that hotel down about ten or eleven years ago.

DONALD: What? No.

BLAKE: I'm pretty sure.

BLAKE: Well, that's a damn shame. It was a lovely hotel. They had a gym. Right there on the ground level. Sometimes I would use the treadmill early in the morning. They had a window that looked out onto the street and I would see the city start to come alive as I worked out.

BLAKE: You see? You could live in a hotel here. A very nice hotel.

DONALD: No. People know where to find me in this location. Mandy said she was going to stop in on her way home from school yesterday. To say hi. She didn't make it though. She must have gotten tied up.

BLAKE: Mandy?

DONALD: Your sister. Yes.

BLAKE: Dad? Mandy doesn't go to school. Mandy is forty-one years old. She's a doctor.

DONALD: . . . I know that. She's a very busy woman. That's why she couldn't visit.

BLAKE: Dad? Are you okay?

DONALD: I'm fine. Also, your mother knows where I am here. I can't be moving from place to place. She'll lose track of me. What if she needs me?

BLAKE: She doesn't need you, Dad. She's got Roger now.

DONALD: . . . Oh, right. I forgot about Roger. Well, that won't last. He's not her type at all.

BLAKE: Why would you say that? Have you met him?

DONALD: No, but I've met other Rogers. Very uppity, Rogers are. Their noses in the air. Your mother likes a more down-to-earth type. No, I give it a month.

BLAKE: They've been together for seven months.

DONALD: And the clock is ticking, believe me.

BLAKE: So, you won't move?

DONALD: No. People know where to find me here. Fans. The press.

BLAKE: The press?

DONALD: Yes. Now, no more talk of moving. Let's just sit here and finish our beer. Spend some one-on-one time together? You know how I like spending time with my son.

BLAKE: I know. Me too, Dad.

After a moment.

DONALD: That scared me.

BLAKE: What did?

DONALD: Thinking Mandy was going to stop by after school. I know she's not in school anymore. Why would I say that?

BLAKE: You just got confused, that's all. It was in the middle of a heated conversation.

DONALD: Yes, that was probably it. She hasn't called, you know.

BLAKE: I know.

DONALD: I'm beginning to think that maybe she won't call at all. Ever.

BLAKE: You're beginning to think? Dad, it's been two years since the breakup.

DONALD: Has it been that long?

BLAKE: Yes. And believe me, I've talked to Mandy. We've had many volatile discussions about her coming to see you. She is adamant.

DONALD: But how can a child do that—cut off all ties with a parent—over a misunderstanding? And that's all it was. A misunderstanding.

BLAKE: She sees it as more than that. She sees how it hurt Mom.

DONALD: Then why doesn't your mother intervene? She's gotten over it, hasn't she? She's moved on. She has that snob Roger.

BLAKE: He's not a snob.

DONALD: Why can't she tell Mandy to get over it?

BLAKE: Dad, Mandy thinks you betrayed her as well.

DONALD: I betrayed no one! It was a complicated matter. I told you that. I was just trying to ease another human being's burden.

BLAKE: You paid her rent for thirty-three years. That's the problem. That's what nobody can understand. Everyone assumes there must be more to it than just easing her burden. They think you must have had a child with this woman or still be in love with her.

DONALD: There was no child! There was no relationship! Why can't you people believe that?

BLAKE: Because you're so mysterious about it.

DONALD: It's complicated.

BLAKE: Yes, you've said that.

DONALD: Well, when you see Mandy, will you tell her I said hi?

BLAKE: I will.

DONALD: And tell her . . . tell her I love her.

BLAKE: I tell her that every time I see her, Dad.

DONALD: You're a good son.

BLAKE: Let me take you out to dinner. My treat. I'm going to buy you a healthy meal for a change. How does that sound?

DONALD: A healthy meal?

BLAKE: Yes.

DONALD: Do I have a choice?

BLAKE: No.

DONALD: Fine. I'll go and get changed.

DONALD gets up.

BLAKE: Why?

DONALD: Well, you're taking me out to a fancy restaurant, aren't you?

BLAKE: Who said fancy? I said healthy.

DONALD: Oh, I don't eat just anywhere, Blake. After all . . .

BLAKE: I know. You're a Pulitzer Prize winner.

DONALD: And don't you forget it.

BLAKE: How can I? You mention it every chance you get.

DONALD: So, what fancy restaurant are we going to?

BLAKE: I'll take you to Monahan's.

DONALD: Ooh, that is fancy. I might even put on a tie.

DONALD moves towards the bedroom. Then he stops.

Oh. The script is in my desk drawer if you want to have a look.

BLAKE: What's that?

DONALD: The script. *Cast in Stone*. You can have a look if you like.

BLAKE: But, I just . . .

DONALD: You just what?

BLAKE: Nothing. I'll have a look.

DONALD: And be brutally honest. I can take it.

DONALD exits to the bedroom. BLAKE moves towards the kitchen, but stops and goes to the desk. He opens a drawer and pulls out the seven pages of script. He looks at the pages for a moment. BLAKE puts the pages back into the desk and exits to the kitchen. Lights down.

SCENE FOUR

Four years ago. July.

Lights come up. BLAKE *enters carrying a birthday cake. He sets the cake on the coffee table.*

BLAKE: Dad? Are you up?

No answer.

Dad?

DONALD: *(off)* Be right out.

BLAKE *lights the one candle that is on the cake.* DONALD *enters.*

BLAKE: Happy birthday!

DONALD: Oh, my. Will you look at this? Look at this. This isn't for me?

BLAKE: Of course it is. Who else's birthday is today?

DONALD: But my birthday is on the seventeenth.

BLAKE: I know.

DONALD: July seventeenth.

BLAKE: Yes, Dad. That's what today is.

DONALD: It is?

BLAKE: Yes.

DONALD: Oh my God. I've been so busy with the . . . with the new— *(points to his desk)* Whatchamacallit.

BLAKE: Your new script?

DONALD: Script. Yes. I guess I lost all track of time.

BLAKE: Well, it's your birthday, so make a wish and blow out the candle.

DONALD: Well, what do you know about that? Isn't this lovely? All right. Here goes.

DONALD blows out the candle.

BLAKE: Good job. So, do you know how old you are?

DONALD: Well, of course I know how old I am. What kind of a fool question is that? I'm seventy-one.

BLAKE: That's right. And how does seventy-one feel?

DONALD: Like someone beat me about the body with a crowbar.

BLAKE: You don't feel well?

DONALD: Oh, nothing serious. Just run down, that's all. I need to get more exercise. There's a gym in this building. I think I'll start going there. Use the treadmill.

BLAKE: A gym? I don't think there's a gym in this building, Dad.

DONALD: Yes, there is. It's on the ground level.

BLAKE: I don't think so.

DONALD: Blake, I'm telling you there's a gym. I've seen it.

BLAKE: All right. I guess I must've missed it.

DONALD: Well, you're never around. How would you see it?

BLAKE: Right. And on that front, I've got some news.

DONALD: Did you want some cake now? I'll get a knife and cut you a piece.

DONALD starts for the kitchen.

BLAKE: No, thanks, Dad. Not right now.

DONALD: Are you sure?

BLAKE: Yes, positive. Come and sit down. I've got some news for you.

DONALD: All right. I hope it's good news. We could all use some good news.

DONALD sits.

BLAKE: Oh, I think it might be.

DONALD: A birthday cake. What do you know about that? Did your mother bake that?

BLAKE: No.

DONALD: We'll have to save a piece for Mandy.

BLAKE: Dad, listen to me. Are you listening?

DONALD: I'm listening. What is it?

BLAKE: I'm moving back home.

DONALD: You're what?

BLAKE: I'm leaving London and coming home.

DONALD: Well, that is good news, son. Very good news. I know your mother will be happy to hear that.

BLAKE: She was very happy to hear it. And what about you?

DONALD: Me? Well, I'm extremely happy to hear it. I want my children around me in my golden years, so of course I'm happy to hear it.

BLAKE: Your children?

DONALD: Yes.

BLAKE: Well, that's not really possible right now, is it?

DONALD: Why not?

BLAKE: Mandy's working in Calgary, Dad.

DONALD: What do you mean?

BLAKE: Mandy took a job as the head of oncology at Rockyview General in Calgary. Six months ago.

DONALD: Oh. Right.

BLAKE: Nobody told you?

DONALD: Oh, I'm sure they did, yes. It's just that I've been so busy with the uh . . .

DONALD points to his desk.

BLAKE: Script?

DONALD: Yes. I just forgot, that's all. And I just woke up from a nap. I'm a little groggy.

BLAKE: You've been sleeping a lot I've noticed.

DONALD: Oh no more than usual, I don't think. Well, good for Mandy. That's quite a step up.

BLAKE: I'll say it is. She's the youngest head of oncology in the country.

DONALD: Oh, she's extremely talented, that one. I'm very proud of her.

BLAKE: So, I'll be moving back at the end of this month.

DONALD: She was valedictorian, you know. When she graduated.

BLAKE: I know that.

DONALD: She's got the Wellner intellect, that one.

BLAKE: So, three more weeks and I'll be moving back home, Dad.

DONALD: Oh, that's wonderful, son. I'm very happy to hear that.

BLAKE: We'll get to spend more time together.

DONALD: Yes. But I still have my work to do. I can't let social commitments take me away from that.

BLAKE: And how's the script coming? Still plugging away at it?

BLAKE moves to the desk and looks at the typewriter.

DONALD: Oh, yes. Every day I do a little work on it. But these things take time. You can't rush it.

BLAKE looks at the paper in the typewriter.

BLAKE: Uh-huh.

DONALD: So, what happened in London?

BLAKE: What do you mean?

DONALD: Why are you moving back? Something must have happened, right?

BLAKE: Well, the job didn't work out. And besides, I've got a book I want to write. So, I thought if I came back here and did some freelance travel writing, I could spend the rest of my time working on the book. And I'd be near you as well.

DONALD: Now, you're not moving back just because of me, I hope.

BLAKE: Well, that's part of the reason. I mean, you're seventy-one now.

DONALD: I can get by quite nicely on my own, Blake. I don't need a babysitter.

BLAKE: Mom says you had a fall last week.

DONALD: A fall?

BLAKE: You got dizzy or something?

DONALD: Oh. That. Well, that was nothing. I'll tell you what that was. That was the Scotch.

BLAKE: Scotch?

DONALD: Yes, I've taken to drinking Scotch. Roman across the hall gave me a taste a while back and I must say I've taken quite a shine to it. Besides, Scotch is a far classier drink for a famous writer than beer, don't you think? Robbie Burns drank Scotch. And Eugene O'Neill too, I think. Would you like a glass? A bit of the ol' John Barleycorn?

BLAKE: No, I'm not a fan of Scotch, Dad.

DONALD: Well, I think I'll have one. The sun is over the yard-arm, right?

DONALD finds a bottle of Scotch somewhere in the room and pours himself a drink.

I drink it "neat" as they say. No ice. No water. Just the Scotch itself. That's how real Scotch drinkers take it.

BLAKE: So, you're saying you fell because you had too much to drink?

DONALD: Yes, I'm ashamed to say that is correct. But it hasn't happened since. It was a one-time occurrence.

BLAKE: How did Mom get involved?

DONALD: Oh, Roman panicked and called an ambulance and I went to the hospital. Your mother is still listed as my emergency contact. Cheers.

DONALD drinks.

BLAKE: Well, you'll have to fix that. You can make me your contact.

DONALD: Yes. That's a good idea. So, you're moving back you say?

BLAKE: At the end of this month, yes.

DONALD: And why are you here now?

BLAKE: I came home for the wedding, Dad. You know that. Plus, I wanted to see you. I've been away for a year. I thought I'd come back. Spend a few days with you.

DONALD: We could watch a football game. Oh, I love football. I watch it all the time with my son.

BLAKE: Pardon me?

DONALD: Football. My son and I watch football every Sunday.

BLAKE: Dad?

DONALD: Yes?

BLAKE: I'm your son.

DONALD: . . . Blake.

BLAKE: Yes.

DONALD: Well, of course you are. I know that. I told you, I just woke up.

BLAKE: And that's why you're confused?

DONALD: Yes. Listen, why aren't you staying with me? I've got a perfectly good pullout couch here. You'd be very comfortable.

BLAKE: I'm staying with Mom because I had to help out with the wedding. They got married in the backyard and I was kind of in charge of decorating the place.

DONALD: Ah. Of course. You have a decorator's eye. You always did. And you say you're not gay.

BLAKE: I'm not gay.

DONALD: Of course you aren't. Well, listen, on your next visit, you stay here with me.

BLAKE: Actually, the next time I'm here, I'll be moving back.

DONALD: Then you can stay here until you find a place of your own. I've got a perfectly good pullout couch here. You'll be very comfortable.

BLAKE: Sounds good.

DONALD: So, you say you're writing a book?

BLAKE: Yes.

DONALD: A restaurant guide?

BLAKE: No, Dad, I haven't done restaurant reviews for a year now. It's going to be a novel.

DONALD: A novel? That's quite the undertaking.

BLAKE: Well, I figured I should give it a shot. And I'm very excited about it. It's about this . . .

DONALD: You didn't leave London on a bad note, I hope.

BLAKE: No. Not at all.

DONALD: Are you sure? Because burning bridges is not good.

BLAKE: I didn't burn any bridges.

DONALD: People have long memories. If you leave a bad impression it'll come back to haunt you, Blake.

BLAKE: I didn't leave a bad impression. I'm leaving on good terms.

DONALD: Well, that's fine then. Good boy.

BLAKE: So, the novel is about this . . .

DONALD: I spent some time in London myself. Of course, that was a long time ago. They were doing *A Kind Heart* there in the West End.

BLAKE: Uh-huh.

DONALD: So much happened during my time there. So much.

BLAKE: You know, I visited Virginia Honeywell's grave while I was there.

DONALD: You what?

BLAKE: It wasn't hard to find. She was fairly well known, as you know. So, I visited her grave. She's up on a hill. All by herself. I thought she might have been buried near her husband, but she wasn't. She was all alone up there. That's kind of sad, don't you think?

DONALD: Very sad, yes. Well, she never remarried. Didn't have children. Had no one in her life as far as I know. She lived out her days alone and I assume it was her choice to be buried up there alone.

BLAKE: Did you keep in touch with her?

DONALD: No. I followed her through her press notices. The occasional interview. I thought it best to keep my distance for various reasons.

BLAKE: Tell me about her.

DONALD: Virginia?

BLAKE: Yes.

DONALD: Well, let's see. She was a beautiful strawberry blond. And a wonderful actress. But more than that, she was a good person. Decent to the core. And authentic. Not a false note about her.

BLAKE: You cared for her very much. You told me that.

DONALD: I did, yes. Perhaps more than I should have, given the outcome. I signed the divorce papers for your mother, you know.

BLAKE: I know you did.

DONALD: She was in some kind of hurry, I'll tell you that much.

BLAKE: Yes, she was.

DONALD: I never thought it would actually come to that, but it just goes to show you how much I know. Oh! That's why you came home. Of course. You're here for the wedding.

BLAKE: That's right.

DONALD: And how was it?

BLAKE: The wedding was lovely.

DONALD: Your mother made a beautiful bride, I'll bet.

BLAKE: She did.

DONALD: Of course she did. Good for her. I remember the day your mother and I got married. She wanted everything to go right. Well, what bride doesn't? And everything did go right, until we exited the church and your mother noticed the photographer at the bottom of the stairs. She didn't want him shooting up like that. She didn't want her wedding picture to be looking up her nostrils. So, she buried her chin in her chest and wound up looking like a hunchback. Well, here. Here it is here. See?

He gets the photo from the bookcase.

It is still my favourite photo of the two of us because it is a microcosm of our relationship. Me, just happy to be standing next to this wonderful woman, and your mother worrying about it not being perfect. I should have known she wouldn't understand.

BLAKE: Wouldn't understand what?

DONALD: That I was paying Virginia's rent. I knew she wouldn't understand.

BLAKE: Then why did you do it?

DONALD: Ah, life is strange sometimes, Blake. Sometimes it pushes you down a road you had no intention of travelling. Was Mandy at the wedding?

DONALD puts the photo back on the bookcase.

BLAKE: Yes, she was.

DONALD: So, she came in from Calgary for it, did she?

BLAKE: Yes.

DONALD: Has she gone back now?

BLAKE: She flew back this morning.

DONALD: Uh-huh. Well, I guess maybe it's time that I . . . uh . . . That I stopped hoping for her to come around. I guess maybe it's time. It's not good for a person's mental state, you know. Holding out hope that way, and then being let down again and again. I don't think it's good for a person.

BLAKE: I'm really sorry about this, Dad.

DONALD: No. Don't be sorry, son. It's my fault entirely. This hasn't caused a rift between you and your sister, I hope.

BLAKE: We get heated about it every so often, but we always make up. We're awfully close, Mandy and me.

DONALD: Good. Good. Because that would break my heart if you two were to have a falling out over something I did.

BLAKE: Something you did? Are you saying you did something now?

DONALD: Yes. I paid that woman's rent for thirty-three years.

BLAKE: Oh. So you're still sticking to that?

DONALD: I'm not sticking to anything. That's all it was. I paid her rent.

BLAKE: Why?

DONALD: To ease her burden.

BLAKE: To ease her burden. That's become a pretty stock answer, Dad.

DONALD: Wait. It's my birthday today.

BLAKE: That's right. It is.

DONALD: Did you get me a present?

BLAKE: Uh . . . no.

DONALD: A card?

BLAKE: I got you a cake.

DONALD: A cake.

BLAKE: Chocolate. Your favourite.

DONALD: That's not good enough. You should have gotten me a present too.

BLAKE: Did anybody else get you anything? Mom? Mandy? Your friend Roman something across the hall?

DONALD: No.

BLAKE: Then I think I'm looking pretty good right now.

DONALD: What was the name of that fancy restaurant you took me to last week?

BLAKE: What fancy restaurant? We didn't go to a restaurant last week.

DONALD: Monahan's. That was it.

BLAKE: That was last year, Dad. Not last week.

DONALD: No, it was last week. And that's where I want to go tonight.

BLAKE: Tonight?

DONALD: Yes. You're here to take me out for my birthday, right? A celebration of my seventy-one years?

BLAKE: Well, if that's what you want.

DONALD: That's what I want. Dinner out with my son.

BLAKE: Okay. Monahan's it is.

DONALD: That's my boy! I'll get changed. Come and help me pick out a tie.

BLAKE: All right.

DONALD exits to the bedroom. BLAKE looks at the typewriter.

Page eight.

BLAKE exits to the bedroom. Lights down.

SCENE FIVE

Three years ago. September.

DONALD enters. BLAKE enters. BLAKE is carrying a suitcase.

DONALD: This is not necessary. I'm fine.

BLAKE: You're not fine, Dad. The doctors are saying we should move you into a home. You've fallen twice in the past year. You forget things.

DONALD: I'm seventy-two. What man of seventy-two doesn't forget things? And so what if I've fallen twice? Twice in a year? That's nothing! With the amount I drink, I should be falling five or six times a week!

BLAKE: Dad. Either I move in with you for a while, or you go to a home.

DONALD: Ahhhhh!

BLAKE: Never mind ahhhh! It's not permanent. I'm just going to keep an eye on you. Monitor you for a couple of weeks and set some kind of regimen for you that you can follow after I leave and you're here by yourself again.

DONALD: What kind of regimen?

BLAKE: Diet for one. Those falls could be due to a lack of something in your diet.

DONALD: Such as?

BLAKE: Magnesium. Or maybe it's due to dehydration. Maybe you're not drinking enough water.

DONALD: What are you, a doctor now?

BLAKE: No, but we have a doctor in the family if you recall. I asked her what it could be.

DONALD: Mandy.

BLAKE: Yes, Mandy.

DONALD: So, was this her idea? You moving in?

BLAKE: It was a suggestion. And it's only for two weeks. I've got my own life. I can't be putting that on hold because you want to be stubborn and not look after yourself. So, are we settled?

DONALD: And it's only for two weeks?

BLAKE: Believe me, that will be more than either of us can stand.

DONALD: All right, fine.

DONALD goes to the Scotch bottle.

BLAKE: What are you doing?

DONALD: I'm having a Scotch.

BLAKE: Have you had any lunch?

DONALD: Not yet.

BLAKE: Then you're not having Scotch. Scotch on an empty stomach is not a good idea. Especially for someone who falls.

DONALD: I'm not someone who falls. I've fallen twice in a year. That's not someone who falls.

BLAKE: Well, it's certainly not someone who doesn't fall.

DONALD: It's someone who tripped. Twice!

BLAKE: Give me that.

BLAKE takes the bottle of Scotch.

We'll have lunch and then you can have a glass of Scotch.

DONALD: This is going to be the longest two weeks of my life.

BLAKE: So, what can I make you?

DONALD: Nothing. I haven't got any food in the apartment.

BLAKE: Why not?

DONALD: I haven't gone shopping.

BLAKE: You see? This is why I need to be here. So, we're going to go grocery shopping. Together. I'm going to show you what you need to buy. In fact, I'll make a list of what you need to buy every week. That's the very first thing we'll do.

BLAKE goes to the desk and gets a pen and a piece of paper. He looks at the typewriter while he's there. He sits and begins making a list.

DONALD: You're going to make me buy healthy stuff with no flavour, right?

BLAKE: Yes. That's exactly right. And I'm going to clean this apartment too. Don't you ever vacuum?

DONALD: I don't have a vacuum.

BLAKE: Then how do you clean the floors?

DONALD: I don't need to. I'm careful not to spill anything.

BLAKE: Okay, we're buying you a vacuum cleaner too. Are you doing laundry? Do you launder your clothes?

DONALD: When I feel like it.

BLAKE: When you feel like it? You're not wearing dirty underwear, I hope.

DONALD: My underwear is fine.

BLAKE: Is it soiled?

DONALD: It's not soiled! Would I sit around in soiled underwear?

BLAKE: I don't know. That's why I'm asking.

DONALD: Well, I wouldn't. I'm not an animal.

BLAKE: What about ironing? Do you need anything ironed?

DONALD: I don't need anything ironed.

BLAKE: Because you don't have to go around in wrinkled clothes.

DONALD: I'm not going around in wrinkled clothes. I'm very particular to buy the best of wash and wear.

BLAKE: All right. Because when you look good you feel good. That's all a part of healthy living.

DONALD: Didn't I write a play about this once? About two men living together who grew to hate each other?

BLAKE: That was Neil Simon, Dad. *The Odd Couple*. And we're not going to grow to hate each other.

DONALD: Wanna bet?

BLAKE: We're going to get you back on the path to a healthy lifestyle.

DONALD: Neil Simon never won a Pulitzer Prize.

BLAKE: Yes, he did. For *Lost in Yonkers*.

DONALD: Oh. Well, I won mine from up here in Canada. Let's see you do that, Neil Simon.

BLAKE: Dad, Neil Simon is dead.

DONALD: Something else I beat him at. Life! So, how's your book coming along?

BLAKE: Almost done. And I've already got a publisher interested.

DONALD: Really?

BLAKE: I sent him the first five chapters and he really liked it.

DONALD: Good for you. And he liked it?

BLAKE: Very much.

DONALD: Excellent. Did you mention my name? That might help, you know? If you mention my name and that you're my son, that could hasten the process along.

BLAKE: No, I didn't mention your name.

DONALD: You didn't?

BLAKE: No. I mentioned Neil Simon's name.

DONALD: Very funny. Why didn't you mention my name?

BLAKE: Because I'd rather get by on my own merits, Dad.

DONALD: Oh, don't be ridiculous. You need every advantage you can get in the literary world. Mention my name, for God's sake.

BLAKE: I will mention your name. If things get bogged down, I'll definitely drop your name.

DONALD: Good. Anything I can do to help.

BLAKE: Thank you. And how's *Cast in Stone* coming along?

DONALD: *Cast in Stone*?

BLAKE: The play you're working on.

DONALD: Oh that. Well, I think it's coming along nicely. Very nicely indeed.

BLAKE: I noticed you're on page ten.

DONALD: It's a slow process, but you can't rush these things.

BLAKE: Yes, I've heard.

DONALD: Tell me more about your book. What's it about?

BLAKE: Oh, it's just a story about a family.

DONALD: A family?

BLAKE: Yes.

DONALD: What family? Not our family?

BLAKE: No, of course not. I mean, what's interesting about our family? Aside from my father paying an actress's rent for thirty-three years, my mother divorcing him and remarrying a man who turned out to be after her money that she got when she divorced my father, and now this gold-digger named Roger is living in a tiki hut somewhere in Bora Bora while my mother has taken to her bed in a state of great grief and shame, and my sister just got married to a scientist slash inventor who's come up with a bow and arrow that can shoot around corners. Write about that family? Why would I want to do that?

DONALD: You're right. We're very ordinary.

BLAKE: So, this is a fictional family. I made them up.

DONALD: Ah, so you're creating finally. Good for you. And how was the wedding?

BLAKE: Mandy's? It was fine. He's actually a very nice guy. Just a little flaky. But Mandy loves him and that's the main thing.

DONALD: Good. I'm sorry I couldn't make it.

BLAKE: You weren't invited.

DONALD: And that's why I couldn't make it. You know, I always looked forward to that day when I would walk Mandy down the aisle. I think every father looks forward to that day. I'm sorry she didn't think that it would mean that much to me.

BLAKE: Mandy is selfish.

DONALD: Oh, don't say that about your sister. I hate hearing you say things like that.

BLAKE: Well, she is, Dad. I'm very annoyed that she hasn't given you a chance after all this time.

DONALD: Ahh. That's all right. So, who walked her down the aisle?

BLAKE: I did.

DONALD: You?

BLAKE: Me.

DONALD: Is that common? A brother giving a sister away at a wedding?

BLAKE: I don't know. And Mandy didn't call it "giving her away." That would imply that she was a possession.

DONALD: Well, what did she call it?

BLAKE: Handing her over.

DONALD: Handing her over? Like she's a satchel of money in a bank heist?

BLAKE: That's how she put it.

DONALD: I tried, you know. I tried to contact Mandy by phone a number of times, but she would just hang up. So, I stopped. Why do we need a bow and arrow that can shoot around corners?

BLAKE: I don't know.

DONALD: This family is nuts.

BLAKE: You know what we need to do? We need to figure out some activities you can do to keep your mind active.

DONALD: What's wrong with my mind?

BLAKE: You're seventy-two. That's what's wrong with your mind. Mandy thinks we should get you on galantamine.

DONALD: What the hell is that?

BLAKE: It's a drug used to treat . . .

DONALD: Treat what?

BLAKE: Mild symptoms of Alzheimer's.

DONALD: Alzheimer's? Don't be ridiculous.

BLAKE: I told her you wouldn't go for it.

DONALD: You're damn right I won't go for it.

BLAKE: Then we need to do some exercises to keep your mind sharp.

DONALD: Like what?

BLAKE: I don't know. How about crossword puzzles?

DONALD: Naw. Too much thinking.

BLAKE: That's the idea! We want you to think. We want you to stretch yourself.

DONALD: I do that when I'm writing.

BLAKE: You're on page ten. Ten pages in four years is not writing. It's doodling. I've got it. I know what we're going to do. We're going to play Scrabble. I'm going to come over a couple of times a week and we're going to play Scrabble. I'll write that down. Buy a Scrabble game.

BLAKE writes.

DONALD: Scrabble with my son. Sweet God in heaven take me now.

BLAKE: Never mind. It'll be good for you. There. The list is done.

DONALD: Mandy said I should take this drug? What's it called?

BLAKE: Galantamine.

DONALD: Mandy said I should take it?

BLAKE: She said you should try it, yes.

DONALD: She's showing an interest in my health?

BLAKE: I asked her for suggestions and she obliged.

DONALD: Then I'll try it.

BLAKE: You will?

DONALD: If Mandy wants me to try it, I'll try it.

BLAKE: Well, we both want you to try it, Dad.

DONALD: Then I will. Now, let's get those flavourless groceries and go to lunch. Then I can have my Scotch. I'll get changed and be right back.

BLAKE: Why are you getting changed? You look fine.

DONALD: I don't know. It's something my father always did. Whenever he went out he would get changed. I guess it's something a gentleman does. I never questioned it. It was like when my father danced with my mother. He would never put the palm of his hand flat against her back because that was considered too familiar. No, it would just be the side of his hand. Thumb and forefinger. Like this.

DONALD demonstrates.

BLAKE: I like that. It's classy.

DONALD: That was my father. Classy to the end. We buried him in a tuxedo. A rental.

DONALD exits to the bedroom. After a moment, we hear a body fall and a groan from DONALD off stage.

BLAKE: Dad? Dad, are you all right?!!

BLAKE exits to the bedroom. Lights down, end Act One.

Act Two

SCENE ONE

Two years ago. November.

A room in the Devon Marsh nursing home. The room has a couch and chairs. There is a small refrigerator in the room. And a kitchen counter. There is a different bookcase, which is filled with photos. There is a small desk that the Underwood typewriter sits on. A Scrabble game sits on the coffee table.

Lights up. DONALD *and* BLAKE *enter. They are wearing dark winter coats.*

BLAKE: Do you think she knows?

DONALD: Knows what?

BLAKE: That we put flowers on her grave every week.

DONALD: It depends on what you believe in. If you believe there is a God and a heaven, then yes, I think she knows. If you believe that we just rot in the ground and are devoured by maggots after we die, then she probably doesn't know and doesn't care.

BLAKE: Congratulations. You've just made me a believer.

DONALD takes his coat off and exits to the bedroom.

I miss her, Dad. I miss her like hell.

DONALD enters. He goes to the counter and pours himself a Scotch.

DONALD: I miss her too, son. I've missed her every day for the last three years.

BLAKE: Five years.

DONALD: What?

BLAKE: You and Mom have been split up for five years.

DONALD: No. Five years? How can I lose track of time like that?

BLAKE: Because you're seventy-three years old and your mind is getting worse by the day. That galantamine isn't helping at all.

DONALD: My mind is fine.

BLAKE: It's not fine, Dad. That's why we moved you in here.

DONALD: Here where?

BLAKE: Here. The Devon Marsh nursing home. You've been here for six months now. And why are you drinking Scotch?

DONALD: Because the sun is over the yardarm.

BLAKE: Oh, so you drink just because it's that time of day?

DONALD: Yes. I'm toasting another tedious revolution of the earth.

BLAKE: Well, don't forget to hide that stuff when I leave. You're not supposed to have alcohol in your room.

DONALD: Oh please. What writer doesn't have alcohol at the ready? Don't these people know who I am?

BLAKE: They know who you are, Dad. You make them aware of it at every turn.

DONALD: And why shouldn't I? I've earned the right.

BLAKE: Yes, you have.

DONALD: Mandy wouldn't even look at me.

BLAKE: What?

DONALD: At the service. Mandy didn't look at me. In fact, she went out of her way not to look at me.

BLAKE: What service?

DONALD: Your mother's funeral service. What the hell service do you think?

BLAKE: Dad, Mom's funeral was four months ago.

DONALD: No, it wasn't. It was . . .

BLAKE: It was four months ago, Dad. Mom died four months ago.

DONALD: Oh.

BLAKE: Mandy's back in Calgary now.

DONALD: I know that. I know.

BLAKE: Why don't you sit down? Come and sit with me.

DONALD: She's the head of oncology there.

BLAKE: Yes, she is.

DONALD: She's very accomplished.

DONALD sits.

Oh, that's better. Walking through a graveyard takes a lot out of a person. Trying not to step on the graves of innocent bystanders. Tiptoeing everywhere. After a few minutes of this you just say "to hell with it," and you walk wherever you want. You're kicking over flowers, besmirching the dead. You don't care anymore. You just want your calves to stop aching.

He sighs.

No, this is much better.

BLAKE: So, have you made any friends here yet?

DONALD: Not yet.

BLAKE: In six months you haven't made one friend?

DONALD: Well, you have to be careful who you let into your life, Blake. There are people out there who wouldn't hesitate to take advantage. And a fellow of my standing, well, I'm a prime target.

BLAKE: Because of your wealth you mean?

DONALD: Exactly. There are swindlers and bounders everywhere. And the staff are the main offenders.

BLAKE: You think the staff would steal from you?

DONALD: In a heartbeat. Why, they wouldn't give it a second thought. No, I have to be vigilant.

BLAKE: Well, vigilant, sure, but I hope you're not getting paranoid.

DONALD: Not at all. Not at all. But I sleep with one eye open.

BLAKE: Do you use the facilities at all? The gym?

DONALD: There is no gym here.

BLAKE: Dad, it's right across the hall.

DONALD: Never seen it.

BLAKE: What about the pool or the hot tub?

DONALD: They closed the hot tub down.

BLAKE: Really? Why?

DONALD: People were having sex in it.

BLAKE: Oh, God.

DONALD: Apparently warm water stimulates whatever needs to be stimulated in old people and they're off to the races. Even if you get into a hot tub without the intention of having sex, it could just wash over you while you're sitting there, and before you know it you're pairing off and having at it.

BLAKE: Oh please.

DONALD: It's true. The woman in the next room told me this.

BLAKE: You've met the woman in the next room?

DONALD: Of course I have. I'm not a recluse. I'm not a snob. Her name is Wendy . . . something.

BLAKE: And she told you about the hot tub shenanigans?

DONALD: Told me? She offered to take me down and show me.

BLAKE: And what happened?

DONALD: It was closed when we got there. Wendy pounded on the door for a few minutes to no avail. And what about you?

BLAKE: What about me?

DONALD: What are you doing for sex?

BLAKE: What?

DONALD: Well, how old are you?

BLAKE: Forty-seven.

DONALD: Forty-seven. You're not married. You have no girlfriend. Or boyfriend that I'm aware of. The last person I remember you dating was that lawyer.

BLAKE: What lawyer?

DONALD: The one that drew up your will.

BLAKE: I wasn't dating him.

DONALD: No?

BLAKE: No.

DONALD: Your mother thought you were.

BLAKE: She did not.

DONALD: We were all set to welcome him into the family.

BLAKE: Dad . . .

DONALD: We were very excited.

BLAKE: Look, I'm not going to talk to my father about my sex life.

DONALD: Why not? A father is supposed to talk about sex with his son.

BLAKE: When the son is twelve! Not when he's forty-seven.

DONALD: So, am I to assume that you're not having sex? That's not good, you know. Keeping all of that stuff bottled up? It could lead to other problems like kidney stones or a gall bladder attack.

BLAKE: Who told you that?

DONALD: Wendy from next door.

BLAKE: Okay, first of all, I think Wendy from next door is after you. Secondly, I am not discussing this topic any further.

DONALD: Why not?

BLAKE: Because the worse your condition gets the less your filter works.

DONALD: What filter?

BLAKE: The filter we all have that tells us not to say certain things out loud.

DONALD: Oh bullshit. What things do I say out loud that I shouldn't?

BLAKE: Inappropriate things.

DONALD: If you think I'm inappropriate you should hear Wendy from next door. She could make a sailor blush.

BLAKE: I'm not surprised.

DONALD: So, you don't want to talk about hot tub sex?

BLAKE: No! I don't want to talk to you about any kind of sex.

DONALD: Well, what do you want to talk about?

BLAKE: Well, you haven't asked about my book.

DONALD: What book?

BLAKE: I wrote a book, Dad.

DONALD: You did?

BLAKE: Yes. I've told you this . . . no, never mind. I know you can't retain a lot of new information anymore. Although you seem to be well-versed on the hot tub. So, yes, I wrote a book. It's called *Lost in the Family Room*.

DONALD: Good title.

BLAKE: And it's selling well.

DONALD: Well, I'm glad to hear that.

BLAKE: So, I guess I'm following in your footsteps.

DONALD: Well, that makes me very happy, Blake. I'm proud of you, son.

BLAKE: Thank you. You said that in kind of a perfunctory fashion.

DONALD: Well, it's what fathers do.

BLAKE: And how's *Cast in Stone* coming along?

DONALD: Cast in what?

BLAKE: *Cast in Stone.* The important play you were working on.

DONALD: Oh. I gave up on that.

BLAKE: You what?

DONALD: I couldn't finish it. I would write pages and pages thinking what I was writing was brilliant, and then I would read it over the next day and it was shit. What I wrote in my many moments of fogginess made no sense in my few moments of clarity. So, I threw it out. It was an embarrassment.

BLAKE: That's okay, Dad. You wrote one great piece of drama and that is more than ninety-nine point nine percent of writers can claim.

DONALD: *A Kind Heart.*

BLAKE: Yes. *A Kind Heart.* So, if you threw it out, what's this?

BLAKE looks at the paper in the typewriter.

DONALD: I don't know.

BLAKE: "Dear Eloise." Dad, what's this?

BLAKE takes the paper out and looks at it.

Is this a poem for Mom?

DONALD: I don't write poetry.

BLAKE: *(reads)* "Dear Eloise, I wanted to say.
I've not been the same since you went away.
I miss you by moments and ache by the hour.
It hurts to exist without you, my flower.
Dear Eloise, I'll come to you soon.
If I get the courage to jump over the moon.
Save me a place somewhere nearby
So close that I can get lost in your eyes."

Did you write this for Mom?

DONALD: It sounds like it.

BLAKE: "I'll come to you soon. If I get the courage to jump over the moon." What does that mean?

DONALD: It's a poem. It doesn't have to mean anything.

BLAKE: You're not thinking of doing something, are you?

DONALD: I think of doing a lot of things. But this place has so many rules I can't do any of them.

BLAKE: Dad, you're not thinking of hurting yourself, are you?

DONALD: Oh, don't be absurd. It's a poem. People say things in poems that they don't mean.

BLAKE: Are you sure?

DONALD: All the time. "I shut my eyes and all the world drops dead."

BLAKE: What?

DONALD: Sylvia Plath. "I shut my eyes and all the world drops dead." Do you think the world really drops dead when she shuts her eyes?

BLAKE: It's not literal. It metaphorical.

DONALD: That's the trouble with poetry. Too many metaphors. Just say what you mean, for God's sake.

BLAKE: Well, this is lovely. Apart from the killing yourself part. And this line here.

DONALD: What line?

BLAKE: "It hurts to exist without you, my flower"?

DONALD: What's wrong with that?

BLAKE: "My flower"? That's kind of hokey, don't you think?

DONALD: Hokey?

BLAKE: Yeah. I think you could do better than that.

DONALD: You're critiquing my work?

BLAKE: No, I'm just saying that one line seems kind of hackneyed.

DONALD: You're critiquing a poem I wrote for my recently deceased ex-wife? The angel who was your mother?

BLAKE: Never mind. I'm sorry I mentioned it.

DONALD: What gives you the right to critique my work? You're not a writer.

BLAKE: I am a writer!

DONALD: A travel writer.

BLAKE: Dad, I wrote a novel. I just told you. Never mind. I'm going to have a glass of that Scotch. God!

BLAKE gets up and pours himself a Scotch.

DONALD: She was a saint, that woman.

BLAKE: I know.

DONALD: And I'm angry. I'm angry that we never got over that speed bump. That I wasn't able to fix that. All that time wasted that could've been spent together. I'll never get that back.

BLAKE: I know, Dad.

DONALD: I never expected to outlive my Eloise. I didn't expect that at all.

BLAKE: Well, they say cancer is the great equalizer. Isn't that what they say? Because it doesn't discriminate. It'll take anybody.

DONALD: She deserved better. She deserved a better life and she deserved a better death.

BLAKE: Dad, let's continue our Scrabble game, okay? Did you make a word?

DONALD: What's that?

BLAKE: Scrabble. After I left the other night. Did you make a word?

DONALD: Oh, yes. Yes. There.

DONALD points. BLAKE looks at the board and reads.

BLAKE: "*Shoizle.*" What's a shoizle?

DONALD: Are you challenging me?

BLAKE: I didn't say that. I'd just like to know what a shoizle is.

DONALD: I don't have to define the word. I just have to put it down. It's up to you to challenge it. Isn't that the rule?

BLAKE: Yes.

DONALD: Well, there you go.

BLAKE: So, you remember the rules of Scrabble but you don't remember that I wrote a book.

DONALD: Well, the rules of Scrabble are important.

BLAKE: Dad?

DONALD: It was a joke. Stop your whining. You sound like a shoizle.

BLAKE: All right. Let's see here.

BLAKE looks at his letters.

DONALD: You were a good son to her, weren't you? To your mother?

BLAKE: I tried, Dad. I think I was, yes.

DONALD: You were both good to her. She loved you and your sister very much.

BLAKE: She did.

DONALD: But she deserved better than me. She deserved better.

BLAKE: Dad, don't talk like that.

DONALD: I should have told her. I almost told her. Many times.

BLAKE: Told her what?

DONALD: About Virginia Honeywell. But I thought it would be too much for her to handle.

BLAKE: What about Virginia Honeywell?

DONALD: Pardon me?

BLAKE: You should have told Mom what about Virginia Honeywell?

DONALD: Oh everything.

BLAKE: That you were having an affair with her? Is that what you should have told Mom?

DONALD: No, no. It was strictly above board. Strictly . . . I don't want to talk about Virginia anymore.

BLAKE: No?

DONALD: No. It happened and that's that. It needn't be discussed.

BLAKE: . . . All right. That's fine. We won't talk about her.

DONALD: I'm sorry.

BLAKE: No, it's okay. We'll continue our Scrabble game.

DONALD: Good.

BLAKE looks at his tiles.

BLAKE: Now, let's see here.

DONALD: You've got crabs.

BLAKE: What?

DONALD: The word "crabs." You've got it in your tiles there.

BLAKE: Oh. You looked at my tiles?

DONALD: Well, you left them alone with me all night. What was I supposed to do?

BLAKE: You were supposed to NOT look at them.

BLAKE puts his tiles down.

All right, there. "Crabs." Twelve points.

DONALD: You also had "braces" for twenty-one points.

BLAKE: Dammit!

BLAKE marks the score.

You're still up by seventeen points. Not bad for a confused old man. Okay, go ahead. Your turn.

DONALD doesn't move.

Dad?

DONALD: . . . I worked out today.

BLAKE: You what?

DONALD: I worked out. In the hotel gym downstairs. They have a window that looks out onto the street. I watched the city come alive.

BLAKE: You did that today? Here?

DONALD: I did.

BLAKE: That's good, Dad. That's good.

DONALD takes a drink of his Scotch and looks out. Lights down.

SCENE TWO

One year ago. November.

Lights up. DONALD *and* BLAKE *enter.* BLAKE *carries a bag of groceries.*

DONALD: I hope you don't mind doing the interview in my hotel room. This is where I feel most at home. The most relaxed.

BLAKE *sets the grocery bag on the counter and begins putting away the groceries.*

I moved in here about . . . oh let's see now . . . about five years ago. I stayed here when they were rehearsing my play up the street, and I became very fond of the place. The staff and I became very close. Yes, that was quite the time. *A Kind Heart.* That was the name of the play. Well, I'm sure you know that. That's why you're interviewing me. I was thirty-three. Thirty-three. A heady time indeed. The world was my oyster. I'm not really sure what that saying means. The world is my oyster. It's from Shakespeare, you know. *The Merry Wives of Windsor.* "The world's mine oyster which I with sword will open." I understand what it means. I'm just not sure why it means that.

He takes a long pause as he thinks.

She was a wonderful woman.

BLAKE: Who was?

DONALD: My wife. Eloise. She had a quality about her. She had . . . she had . . .

BLAKE: Grit?

DONALD: Grit! She had that Wellner grit! She was a fighter!! My God, was she ever. Did you know her? Eloise?

BLAKE: I did.

DONALD: She would have been here for the interview but she, uh . . .

BLAKE: She died.

DONALD: She's shopping, I think. She loves to shop. But not for herself. She buys things for the kids. Mandy and Blake. She spoils them rotten. I keep telling her that. But that's her way. Generous to a fault. What are you doing over there?

BLAKE: I'm putting your groceries away.

DONALD: Oh, you don't have to do that. I have people who do that sort of thing. They come in and they clean and they . . . they put things away. Sometimes I think they steal from me. Not all of them, mind you. But there are a couple that I don't trust. Things go missing. My liquor for one. I can't tell you how many times I go to my liquor cabinet and find that I'm all out.

BLAKE pulls a bottle of Scotch out of a bag.

BLAKE: Would you like a drink now?

DONALD: You know, I think I would. I think I would. The sun is over the yardarm, so let's have one. Pour yourself one too.

BLAKE takes two glasses out of the cupboard and pours two drinks. He gives a drink to DONALD and then begins writing on sticky notes and putting them on objects.

It's mainly the Brazilians I don't trust. They have a culture steeped in shadiness. I don't know why that is. They should be happy. Content. It's warm there. They have colourful clothing. Burros. You know, mules. They have mules. I'd be happy if I had a mule. Who wouldn't be?

BLAKE: Dad, you can't say that about Brazilians. You can't say they're shady.

DONALD: Why not?

BLAKE: Because you're generalizing about a people. It's racist.

DONALD: I'm not talking about all Brazilians. I'm talking about two of them. Ramone and Camila.

BLAKE: Oh. Do they work here?

DONALD: I hope so. They load me into the bathtub every night. But for the most part the staff here at the Embassy West is helpful in every way. And forthright. Very forthright.

BLAKE: The Embassy West Hotel was torn down fifteen years ago, Dad.

DONALD: What was?

BLAKE: The Embassy West Hotel. It's gone.

DONALD: Gone? Nonsense. I was talking to the concierge only this morning. William is his name. Splendid fellow.

BLAKE: William is a nurse here, Dad. You're in a nursing home. The Devon Marsh Home. You've been here for two years now.

DONALD: A nursing home?

BLAKE: Yes.

DONALD: . . . I know that. I've been here for two years now.

BLAKE: That's right.

DONALD: . . . You think I'm losing my mind, don't you?

BLAKE: Yes, I do. That's why I put sticky notes everywhere. So you'll know where everything is.

DONALD: I am not losing my mind. I forget things, sure. But what man of my age doesn't? But, on the whole, I am as sharp as a tack.

BLAKE: If you say so.

DONALD: I do. I do say so. You wait until Eloise gets back. She'll tell you.

BLAKE: Actually, she won't. Because she can't.

DONALD: Oh, she will. You just wait.

BLAKE: So, you've got five apples in there. You've got some cheese. The havarti that you like. I'll slice that up for you before I leave.

DONALD: No, I can do that. Don't be silly.

BLAKE: No, you can't Dad. No sharp knives. That's the rule. I'll cut it up for you. I brought my own knife.

DONALD: Rules. This hotel is fraught with rules.

BLAKE: I bought you some grapefruit juice. Some pineapple slices. Some tangerines.

DONALD: That's a lot of fruit. I won't be getting scurvy, that's for sure.

BLAKE: The fruit is just for between meals. You get your protein and your vegetables at mealtime. In the dining room.

DONALD: If nothing else I'll be regular.

Pause.

You're Blake.

BLAKE: Very good, Dad. Yes. I'm Blake.

DONALD: What about Mandy? Where is she?

BLAKE: She couldn't make it today.

DONALD: She's my favourite.

BLAKE: I know she is.

DONALD: Always has been.

BLAKE: I'm aware.

DONALD: She can do no wrong.

BLAKE: Never.

DONALD: Why couldn't she make it? Is she in school?

BLAKE: She's forty-five, Dad, so no, she's not in school. She's in Calgary with her husband. And even if she was here, she wouldn't come to see you because she can't stand to be in the same room with you.

DONALD: That was a hurtful thing to say. Why would you say something like that?

BLAKE: Because I know that in five minutes you will have forgotten I said it.

DONALD: She's studying to be a doctor.

BLAKE: She is a doctor. And a very good one.

DONALD: Oh, I don't doubt it. She's got a good head on her shoulders that girl. Very smart. She's the success story in our family without question. I mean, sure, I've got the Pulitzer Prize, but she is the real success story.

BLAKE: Okay, Dad, I'm going to record our conversation, all right?

BLAKE takes a small recording device out and sets it on the table.

DONALD: Certainly. And your name is?

BLAKE: Blake.

DONALD: And you write for which publication, Mr. Blake?

BLAKE: Not Mr. Blake. Just Blake. And I don't work for a newspaper. I'm writing your memoirs. I'm a writer. And I'm doing your biography because I think you've had an interesting life and maybe people will want to read about it. Especially if it's written by your son.

DONALD: Blake.

BLAKE: That's right.

DONALD: That's my son. He writes a food column.

BLAKE: No, he's a novelist now. I'm a novelist. And I'm writing your biography. Some would say that I'm cashing in on your fame and I wouldn't disagree.

DONALD: I won the Pulitzer Prize.

BLAKE: And even in your addled state you won't let me forget that. So, I'm going to record our conversation. Okay?

DONALD: You've written a book before?

BLAKE: Yes, I have.

DONALD: What about?

BLAKE: It's about a dysfunctional family. Because that's what I know best.

DONALD: Wonderful. I would never attempt a novel. Too much work. So, kudos to you, sir.

BLAKE: Okay, here we go. Now, during our last session we stopped when you had arrived in London for the West End production of *A Kind Heart*. Do you remember that?

DONALD: London? Oh yes. Yes. Like it was yesterday.

BLAKE: So, tell me about it.

DONALD: Oh, that was a very special time. London was a high point for me. Everybody says Broadway is the mecca for a writer, but to me the West End of London . . . that's when you know you've made it. And the accolades were bountiful. I was the toast of the town.

BLAKE: Did you enjoy that?

DONALD: Oh yes. Very much so. Recognition is like a drug. You can't get enough of it. My, yes. I loved the attention.

BLAKE: So, the play was a hit over there?

DONALD: It was a huge hit. We broke box office records. And we had a wonderful all-British cast. So talented. Brian Forsythe. Allan Hewitson . . .

BLAKE: And Virginia Honeywell?

DONALD: Yes. Yes. Virginia Honeywell. She was a beautiful strawberry blond.

BLAKE: Did you want to talk about her?

DONALD: Well, I don't see why not.

BLAKE: It won't upset you?

DONALD: Oh, goodness no. No, she was a very talented woman. She commanded the stage. A wonderful actress.

He pauses.

BLAKE: Go on.

DONALD: I cared for her very much. But she had a brute of a husband.

BLAKE: Virginia did?

DONALD: An awful man. Horrible fellow. He would be abusive to Virginia quite often. Physically abusive.

BLAKE: I didn't know that.

DONALD: He would hit her. But not in the face, because her face was her fortune and her fortune supported his gambling addiction. So, he would hit her on the body. She showed me the bruises once. It was horrifying.

BLAKE: And this was during rehearsals?

DONALD: Yes. It was a terrible mental strain on the poor girl. She would have crying spells every day. But of course I was the only one who knew the cause of these breakdowns. She confided in me for some reason. Maybe because she saw how attracted I was to her. I don't know. At any rate, we became fast friends. I wouldn't mind some of that cheese now.

BLAKE: All right. I'll get the knife.

BLAKE gets up and gets the knife from his coat pocket.

And Virginia wouldn't leave her husband?

DONALD: Pardon me?

BLAKE: Virginia Honeywell. She wouldn't leave her husband?

DONALD: No. She was afraid to. She was a well-known actress. Her work was highly publicized. She knew he would find her wherever she went and the abuse would start all over again.

BLAKE: That's a shame.

BLAKE goes to the fridge.

DONALD: It was a hopeless situation. Completely beyond repair. So that's why I had to kill him.

BLAKE stops and thinks for a moment.

BLAKE: . . . What?

DONALD: I wouldn't mind some of that cheese now. Did you say you had cheese?

BLAKE: You killed him?

DONALD: Killed who?

BLAKE: Virginia Honeywell's husband.

DONALD: Oh, yes. Yes.

BLAKE: How?

DONALD: Pushed him off a cliff.

BLAKE: Pushed him off a . . . where?

DONALD: Beachy Head. About seventy-five miles south of London. A lovely spot. Virginia and her husband had rented a cottage there for the weekend.

BLAKE: . . . Yes? Keep going.

DONALD: Oh. You'd like to hear more?

BLAKE: Yes. I really would.

DONALD: Well, Virginia had just found out that he had gambled away most of their savings and she was hoping to talk some sense into him about his gambling problem. She thought a romantic getaway might be the place to do it. Which makes no sense to me, but what do I know of romance? Did you say we had cheese?

BLAKE: Yes. I'll get that in a minute.

DONALD: I'm partial to havarti.

BLAKE: Yes. So, they rented a cottage. And then what?

DONALD: Oh, I guess he flew into a rage when she broached the topic of his gambling and he began beating her again. Then, exhausted from the beating, he fell asleep and Virginia called me to tell me what had happened.

BLAKE: And what did you do?

DONALD: I got in my car and drove to the cottage intent on taking her back to London and away from the cad.

BLAKE: But that's not what happened.

DONALD: No. Far from it.

BLAKE: Well, what did happen?

DONALD: Well, when I arrived, I saw Calvin—that was his name, Calvin—I saw Calvin standing near the cliffs overlooking the

English Channel. He had awakened from his nap, I guess, and had gone out for a cigarette. I can still see his silhouette set against the moonlit sky. Smoke wafting up. It was very striking.

BLAKE: . . . Yes? And then what?

DONALD: I stopped the car and approached him, fully intending to scold him severely for his conduct. But the closer I got to him the angrier I became. I called his name and he turned to look at me. And recognizing me, he held up his hand and waved. He was being quite friendly.

BLAKE: And what did you do?

DONALD: I pushed him off the cliff. I put both my hands firmly on his chest and over he went. Five hundred feet straight down. Those cliffs are sheer. They really should have safety barriers.

BLAKE: My God. You actually pushed him off a cliff?

DONALD: With vigour.

BLAKE: Oh my God.

DONALD: And then I heard a scream.

BLAKE: Calvin screamed?

DONALD: No. It came from behind me. Virginia was looking out the cottage window. She'd seen the whole thing. Did you say we had cheese?

BLAKE: All right! Yes. I'm getting the cheese!

BLAKE opens the fridge and takes out the unopened cheese.

And what happened after Virginia saw you push her husband off the cliff? Oh Jesus!!

BLAKE lunges and grabs the recording device and turns it off.

DONALD: Is the interview over?

BLAKE: Yes. For now.

DONALD: It's stuffy in here. I'm going to open the door.

DONALD moves to open the door. BLAKE stops him.

BLAKE: No! You can't open the door!

DONALD: What?

BLAKE: You can't open the door. Ever again! Now come back and sit down.

DONALD sits.

So, what happened after Virginia saw you . . . you know??

BLAKE sits with a plate and slices the cheese.

DONALD: Well, we talked for a while and decided that we would say that Calvin threw himself off the cliff because he was despondent over losing their money.

BLAKE: A suicide.

DONALD: I had a high school friend who tried to commit suicide. Alex Veitch. He threw himself into a neighbour's pool. He was going to drown himself. But it turned out he was too good a swimmer, so he just swam around for an hour and then climbed back out again.

BLAKE: So, you and Virginia decided to say that her husband committed suicide.

DONALD: Yes. The problem was, if it was suicide, Virginia would get none of the insurance money. Whereas if it was . . .

BLAKE: Murder?

DONALD: Then she would get compensation.

BLAKE: But if it was murder then there would be an investigation.

DONALD: And who knows what they would find.

BLAKE: They might find the truth.

DONALD: And we couldn't have that now, could we? You know, we probably shouldn't include this in the memoirs.

BLAKE: So, because she couldn't get any insurance money, you decided to pay her rent for her.

DONALD: Yes.

BLAKE: And whose idea was that?

DONALD: Hers. But it only seemed fair. I mean I did kill her husband.

BLAKE: Shh! Dad, you can't say that.

DONALD: But that's what happened.

BLAKE: Yes, but you can't keep saying it. And you can't tell anybody else this, okay?

DONALD: Tell anybody else what?

BLAKE: About you and Virginia Honeywell's husband.

DONALD: Of course not. No. Mum's the word.

BLAKE: So, this is why you couldn't tell Mom the real reason why you paid Virginia Honeywell's rent for thirty-three years.

DONALD: Yes. But now I don't know if it was worth it. I lost my wife and I lost my daughter. But I couldn't have them think I was a murderer, could I? Even though my reasons for the crime were noble. It was a moral dilemma.

DONALD picks up a piece of cheese.

BLAKE: Oh my God. I have to tell Mandy. No, I can't tell Mandy. I can't tell anyone. Or can I? Can I? I don't know what to do. No. I can't tell anybody. This has got to stay right here.

DONALD: So, you're writing a book? About me?

BLAKE: What? Oh! Yes.

DONALD: Well, isn't that something? I certainly hope I can make my life sound compelling enough for a book.

BLAKE: I think you have.

DONALD: This cheese is wonderful.

BLAKE: I have to tell Mandy. I have to.

BLAKE takes out his phone and dials a number.

DONALD: Havarti with an infusion of jalapeno, am I right? Of course I'm right. And it's got just enough bite to it. I would have to say that this is my favourite of all the cheeses.

BLAKE: *(to the phone)* Mandy? Call me back as soon as you get this message.

DONALD: I wonder why nobody comes to interview me.

BLAKE: What's that?

DONALD: Nobody comes to interview me anymore. Why do you think that is?

BLAKE: Well, you haven't written anything in a long time, Dad.

DONALD: When people came to interview me—newspapers, magazines—it made me feel like I was somebody. That was approval for me. I liked that because that was something I never got from my parents. Approval. Don't get me wrong. I felt loved. That wasn't an issue. But I was never made to feel special. They never lavished praise on me, my parents. When I did something wrong, I would hear about it. Oh boy would I ever. Especially from Dad. But if I did something right, it was as if it was expected of me. And there was no praise. A person can't go through life without the occasional introduction to praise. And to be interviewed, well, that always made me feel very special. But nobody comes around anymore. You're the first one in a very long time.

BLAKE: Well, that might be a good thing under the circumstances.

DONALD: No, I want them to come around. I do.

BLAKE: Yes, but you can't talk about Virginia Honeywell's husband.

DONALD: Oh, no. Of course not. Mum's the word.

BLAKE: Good.

DONALD: So, is this interview over?

BLAKE: Yes it is.

DONALD: Then I think I'll lie down. I'm tired.

BLAKE: That's a good idea, Dad.

DONALD: You make yourself at home, Mr. Blake.

BLAKE: It's not Mr. Blake. It's . . .

DONALD exits to the bedroom. BLAKE's phone buzzes. He answers it.

Mandy? Mandy, listen. I've got something to tell you and you cannot tell another living soul.

Lights down.

SCENE THREE

The present. October.

Lights up. DONALD *and* BLAKE *enter.* BLAKE *carries a book, a notepad, and a bag.*

BLAKE: I want to thank you for this opportunity, Mr. Wellner. It's a privilege being the first one to interview you about your biography.

DONALD: My biography?

BLAKE: It just came out yesterday. I brought you a copy.

BLAKE *hands the book to* DONALD. DONALD *looks at it and reads the title.*

DONALD: *Over the Yardarm: The Life of Donald Wellner.* By Blake Wellner. Well, what do you know about that? Blake is my son's name.

BLAKE: Yes, sir, it is. That's who wrote the book.

DONALD: Blake? Oh, no. No. Blake writes a food column for the *Herald.* He's very uh . . . He struggles to make ends meet.

BLAKE: Well, he wrote this book.

DONALD: Did he?

BLAKE: Yes. And I thought you might like to have a look at it.

DONALD: What's in the bag?

BLAKE: Scotch, sir.

DONALD: So, you come bearing gifts. A book and a bottle of Scotch. Aren't you the crafty one trying to get on my good side.

BLAKE: Would you like a glass?

DONALD: I don't mind if I do. Yes. Thank you. Neat, please. I take it neat.

BLAKE pours the drink for DONALD and gives DONALD the glass.

I have a daughter too.

BLAKE: I beg your pardon?

DONALD: I have a daughter. Mandy? Yes. She's the success story of the family. She's a doctor. A very smart woman. Very bright.

BLAKE: Do you see her?

DONALD: Mandy?

BLAKE: Yes.

DONALD: She was here this morning.

BLAKE: Was she?

DONALD: Just before you got here, in fact. Oh, she loves her old man. A father-daughter relationship is very special.

BLAKE: You must feel very lucky.

DONALD: . . . Or maybe she wasn't here. I forget things sometimes. Or I imagine things. Or so I'm told. So maybe Mandy wasn't here.

BLAKE: No, she was here.

DONALD: She was?

BLAKE: She was. She flies in from Calgary and visits you once a month.

DONALD: Mandy does?

BLAKE: Yes, sir.

DONALD: . . . She's my pride and joy, that one.

BLAKE: I know she feels the same way about you.

DONALD: It took a while but we worked things out. I knew she couldn't stay mad at her old man for long.

BLAKE: Yes. It's a good thing you're just a murderer and not a cheater.

DONALD: I haven't seen Blake in a while though.

BLAKE: You haven't?

DONALD: He moved away to London.

BLAKE: Yes, but he came back.

DONALD: No. No, I don't think he did.

BLAKE: No, I'm pretty sure he did, sir. He came back and he wrote this book about you.

DONALD: Who did?

BLAKE: Blake. Your son.

DONALD: No. No, that wasn't him.

BLAKE: Sir, look. His name is right there on the cover.

BLAKE shows DONALD the book.

DONALD: He was in London last I heard. So, you're here to interview me?

BLAKE: Yes, I am.

DONALD: Good. About *A Kind Heart*?

BLAKE: No, not entirely about that.

DONALD: About winning the Pulitzer Prize?

BLAKE: Well, I'm sure we'll touch on that, but I wanted to talk more about the book.

DONALD: The book?

BLAKE: This book. Your biography.

DONALD: I haven't read it.

BLAKE: Well, I just gave it to you. But you will read it eventually?

DONALD: I don't read books.

BLAKE: But this one is written by your son.

DONALD: Oh! Don't tell the staff here that I have a bottle of Scotch. If you do, they'll steal it from me.

BLAKE: I won't tell.

DONALD: Thank you. They're trustworthy for the most part, the staff, but there are one or two that lean towards the devious.

BLAKE: Your secret is safe with me, sir.

DONALD: Good man.

BLAKE: Well, I'll just leave the book on your desk for you.

DONALD: No, don't leave it there. I work there. It will be in the way.

BLAKE: All right then. I'll leave it here.

BLAKE sets the book down somewhere else in the room.

You can look at it whenever you get a minute. Or not. Whatever you like. Now, is it okay if I record this interview?

DONALD: Yes. Yes. By all means.

BLAKE: Good.

BLAKE puts the recording device on the coffee table.

DONALD: I'm sorry my wife couldn't be here. Eloise. She has a concert this evening. She's a singer. A real talent.

A slight pause.

No, I haven't seen Blake in a very long time. He must've gone away somewhere.

BLAKE: No, I don't think he did.

DONALD: He travels a lot. Too much actually. But, that's his job.

BLAKE: I think he's still around, Mr. Wellner.

DONALD: Please don't contradict me, young man. I think I should know where my own son is.

BLAKE: I'm sorry.

DONALD: He's in London. He writes a travel column.

BLAKE: . . . Let me stop this for a second.

BLAKE turns the recording device off.

DONALD: Is the interview over?

BLAKE: No. I just want to say something before we get started. I want to say something to you while there is still a little bit of Donald Wellner left in there. A little bit of my father behind those eyes. Dad . . . I come here to see you almost every day. I come and I interview you over and over again because it makes you feel important. Because you like the attention. And because I love you. I come and I watch the football games with you on Sunday afternoon. Sometimes I sit and I have dinner with you in the dining room. Or we sit in here and have a Scotch together from a bottle that I smuggle in like I did today. And I don't even like Scotch. We talk about Mom. We talk about Mandy. We talk about your Pulitzer Prize. We talk about *A Kind Heart*. The only thing we don't talk about is me. Because you think I've gone away. Well, I haven't gone away, Dad. I'm right here. I'm Blake. This—

BLAKE goes to the bookcase and takes out a photo.

This was me in little league. I was thirteen years old there. Do you remember that?

DONALD takes the photo.

DONALD: That's Blake.

BLAKE: Yes. That's Blake. That's me. Your son. And now I think I need to say goodbye, Dad, because you're leaving us. Bit by bit. A little bit more each day. And I want you to know that you were a good father to me. I've got no complaints. And I think I was a good son. And I miss you, Dad. Every time I come here to interview you, I miss you. But I will continue to come here and interview you as if it was forty-two years ago and *A Kind Heart* has just opened. I will. I promise. But I have to say goodbye to you now while there is still enough of you in there to understand. And I pray to God there is. Do you understand any of this, Dad?

DONALD doesn't answer.

All right then. Let's get back to the interview.

BLAKE turns the recording device on.

DONALD: You're Blake.

BLAKE: Yes. I'm Blake.

DONALD: You're my son.

BLAKE: That's right, Dad. I'm your son.

DONALD: You've come back.

BLAKE: Yes.

DONALD: I love you, son.

BLAKE: And I love you, Dad.

DONALD: . . . Do me a favour.

BLAKE: Yes?

DONALD: When you leave, hide that bottle of Scotch, because if the staff finds it, that'll be the last of it.

BLAKE: I will. I'll hide it before I go.

DONALD: Good. Good lad. And which publication are you from?

BLAKE: I'm from the *Times*, sir.

DONALD: The *Times*? My my. I'm moving up in the world.

BLAKE: Yes, you certainly are, sir. Now, how old were you when *A Kind Heart* opened on Broadway?

DONALD: I was thirty-three. Thirty-three years old. Those were heady times. Heady times indeed. The world was my oyster.

Lights down. End of play.

CHRONOLOGY

Act One

Scene one: Seven years ago. Donald is sixty-eight. Blake is forty-two. Mandy is thirty-nine.

Scene two: Six years ago. Donald is sixty-nine. Blake is forty-three. Mandy is forty.

Scene three: Five years ago. Donald is seventy. Blake is forty-four. Mandy is forty-one.

Scene four: Four years ago. Donald is seventy-one. Blake is forty-five. Mandy is forty-two.

Scene five: Three years ago. Donald is seventy-two. Blake is forty-six. Mandy is forty-three.

Act Two

Scene one: Two years ago. Donald is seventy-three. Blake is forty-seven. Mandy is forty-three.

Scene two: One year ago. Donald is seventy-four. Blake is forty-eight. Mandy is forty-five.

Scene three. The present. Donald is seventy-five. Blake is forty-nine. Mandy is forty-six.

Acknowledgements

With thanks to Joan Miller, Steve Watts, Kirsten Koza, and Doctor Allan Patrick.

Norm Foster has written sixty plays and has been produced all over the world from Newfoundland to Australia. His most popular plays include *The Melville Boys*, *The Ladies Foursome*, *Hilda's Yard*, and *On A First Name Basis*. He has been given the Los Angeles Drama-Logue Award for *The Melville Boys*, and *The Motor Trade* won the best new play award at the Hollywood NAACP Awards in 2012. He was made an Officer of the Order of Canada in 2017.

First edition: November 2020
Printed and bound in Canada by Rapido Books, Montreal

Jacket illustration and design by Patrick Gray

PLAYWRIGHTS CANADA PRESS
202-269 Richmond St. W.
Toronto, ON
M5V 1X1

416.703.0013
info@playwrightscanada.com
www.playwrightscanada.com
@playcanpress